How Great Thou Art

How Great Thou Art

Stories of God's blessing at Great Wood over the past seventy-five years

COMPILED BY

BILL AND ELIZABETH CARTER

THE CHOIR PRESS

First published in the United Kingdom in 2018 by
The Choir Press

ISBN 978-1-911589-46-4

Contents

This book was published in 2018 to mark the seventy-fifth anniversary of camping at Great Wood.

Extracts from *The Great Wood Story* by John Inchley and Alan Martin (Scripture Union, 1990) have been used with kind permission. All quotes from the book are in italics.

Throughout the book there are contributions from many people who have been involved in the Great Wood story over the years, collated by Bill and Elizabeth Carter.

In addition we wish to acknowledge and thank:

All who have provided material and whose names are recorded in the list of contributors (see appendix 3),

The Choir Press and Harriet Evans for their assistance in presentation and publication,

John and Jan Simmons, David Whitehouse, Lucy d'Orton-Gibson and Lisa Drury for proofreading,

Gerry Nichols and Andy Bennett for technical input,

John Axford and Richard Ascough for use of their archive material.

Introduction

⁓⟨∘⟩⁓

In her book *Quantock Country* (Westaway, 1952), Berta Lawrence refers to hundreds of years of prayers said by the monks of Athelney Abbey, just below Adscombe Farm, having left their mark on the area. It is a very special place and it is rumoured that their prayers echo on in the murmuring of the stream in Seven Wells Combe.

John Inchley's introduction to *The Great Wood Story* in 1990 sets the scene well.

> *Great Wood Camp can only be described as something out of a storybook. It was built especially with children from eight to twelve in mind, though it seems that teenagers and adults are equally captivated by its enchantments.*
>
> *Undoubtedly the best way to discover the camp is on foot, either over the hills and along Seven Wells Combe, or by way of the narrow road which winds and wanders past the cottages in the hamlet of Adscombe. Following the latter course is more direct, and the only way to reach the camp by motor car. After passing Adscombe Farm on the left at the bottom of the combe, the country lane becomes a forestry track which was originally very narrow but was widened and surfaced in 1964. After surmounting a steep rise on this track one cannot help being fascinated by the view which meets the eye. On the right, at the very edge of the roadway, there rises a precipitous hill covered with conifer trees, while across the narrow valley, on the opposite side, there are other hills with more and more trees – hundreds and thousands of them – larches, pines and firs. These are the beginnings of 2,000 acres of open forest where the red deer and other wild creatures can often be seen wandering through the trees. There are usually buzzards hovering, with their broad wings outstretched, high in the sky, their mewing cries betraying their constant presence. The smaller birds inhabit the hedgerows according to the season of the year.*

In less than a mile is the gate to the camp field on the left-hand side where the first thing that strikes the newcomer is the well-spaced semi-circle of six beautiful sleeping cabins with staggered roofs on the far side of the field.

Behind the cabins, and near enough to them to be usable, flows a sizeable trout stream which can be enjoyed in all sorts of fascinating ways and which forms the eastern boundary of the camp field. The stream's musical murmurings are never silent, and it, along with the 'tak two coos tak two' cries of the wood-pigeons in the forest, provides one of the two sounds which every camper remembers when he or she thinks of Great Wood. At the end of the field, if one looks down the valley across the camp-fire site and the swimming pool, glimpses can sometimes be caught of the Bristol Channel in the far distance. At the opposite end, beyond the flag mast, large banks of rhododendron almost completely hide a most attractive open-air chapel. It has the stream with its constant music on two of its sides and is reached across a bridge and through a wrought iron gate.

Facing the cabins, on the far side of the field, is an equally beautiful cedar wood mess hut and kitchen, while beyond the mess hut are the camp shop and two ablution areas with hot and cold running water. There is also a comparatively new hut for indoor games and sleeping accommodation for helpers. At the opposite end of the field, behind a hedge and a gate, is sited the Banda hut which is usually occupied by the leader of the camp with his or her family.

Beyond the 2,000 acre forest are the undulating Quantock Hills waiting to be explored, stretching for twelve miles or so from south-east to north-west and almost reaching the sea at Quantoxhead and St Audries. The hills have wooded and steep-sided valleys, many of them with deciduous trees which provide coverts for the red deer. The valleys are called combes – having such delightful names as Butterfly Combe, Hodder's Combe, Lady's Combe and Cockercombe. The hills also have enchanting names – Wills Neck, Longstones, Higher and Lower Hare Knap, Robin Upright's and Hurley Beacon. There are sombre and more macabre names too, such as Dead Woman's Ditch and Walford's Gibbet. When the weather is clear enough there are magnificent views of Flat Holm and Steep Holm in the Bristol Channel with the coast of South Wales in the far distance.

In many places the hills, which are not more than 1,261 feet high, are covered with whortleberries called 'whorts', and are resplendent in the autumn with heather and ling. The principal trees are beech and holly with large areas of oak scrub. Depending on the season primroses, bluebells, foxgloves, rosebay willow-herb and even yellow broom lend luxuriant colour to the sides of the combes while there are breath-taking tracts of wild rhododendron blooms here and there in May and June. The area is ideal for exploring, having picnics, orienteering and enjoying wide games by day or by night. All this may explain why Great Wood has come to be, by common consent, a children's paradise, to which the helpers as well as the boys and girls find themselves compulsively returning over and over again.

The camp, however, has not always been as it is now, though the surroundings are the same and it has perpetually had the same drawing power for young and old alike. In the following pages an attempt is to be made to describe its beginnings in the 1940s with its gradual development over the years.

One of the chief reasons for writing this record is to acknowledge God's goodness, not only at the beginning but ever since, and it needs to be made perfectly clear that this is so.

This would be acknowledged as the motivation for updating the book too. God is the same yesterday, today and for ever.

1940s: Beginnings

*T*he establishment of Great Wood as an adventure camp originally for junior schoolboys was probably a reaction on my part towards the generally accepted leisure time activities of schoolboys attending Christian camps in the late 1930s.

The value of adventure camping for character building was also to be discovered by the instigators of the Duke of Edinburgh's Awards. Although these did not become realities until 1956 they were the outcome of the convictions in the 1940s of Kurt Hahn, who was the founder and first headmaster of Gordonstoun. The setting up of the first Outward Bound School for older boys at Aberdovey in 1941 was another development of this. The founders of the camp at Great Wood with younger boys in mind were, however, entirely ignorant of these bold innovations at that time, and were, if anything, following in the footsteps of Baden Powell, who had already dreamed up such adventurous procedures as early as 1907 when he had commenced the movement called Boy Scouts.

It was in fact my involvement with two lively Scout troops, first at Highgate Junior School and then at Monkton Combe Junior School, which confirmed to me the tremendous value of enterprise and adventure. I was, at the time, feeling the strain of the war years and it was decided that I should indulge myself for the inside of a week in a holiday of horse-riding, my favourite activity at the time. But my scouts at Monkton Combe had an active tradition of camping, and it was also important for me to find a site for their camp which had already been promised for the beginning of the school's summer holidays. When I was not on the back of a horse I managed to borrow a bicycle and found myself negotiating with farmers concerning suitable camping sites. I had almost decided to go to a farm near St Audries but realised that I was not altogether happy with the arrangements. I shared my misgivings with Jack House, who owned the riding stables at Nether Stowey at that time. Mr House's reply was that there was a field at Over Stowey, in Seven Wells Combe, where he had seen campers from time to time. He also said that they were going hunting the next day and

1

passing the place. I was leaving in the afternoon but readily agreed with Mr House's suggestion that there could be a horse ready saddled for me in the morning, and that Mr House would show me the field. All happened as planned and looking back it seems extremely fitting that the field which was to be Great Wood Camp should be approached first of all on horseback. I was shown the spot by Jack House and was greatly attracted by it. It had all the essentials for a good campsite and was nearer the trains at Bridgwater; it was also in itself much more accessible than the St Audries site. I, therefore, mounted the horse again, which I had left tethered to the gate while I explored, and set off to find the farmer. Mr Sydney Tucker, as the farmer's name turned out to be, was a big man and straight as a die. Later on it was discovered that he with his wife and all of his family were very wonderful Christians, though I did not know it at the time. Mr Tucker, however, was agreeable for his field to be used for camping and, there and then, an agreement was entered into. I eventually left the horse at the stables, and went home extremely happy with myself.

So it came about that the Scouts at Monkton Combe Junior School were the first of many boys, and later on girls as well, to savour the delights of Great Wood, as the camp came to be called. There were twenty in all, camping under canvas from July 27 to August 4 1943; they were the pioneers of what was to become a permanent camp, though they were ignorant of this at the time. Many of these original campers and/or their children still have association with the camp.

The First Great Wood Camp ... Ever

Michael Owen remembers a form teacher who came down to Monkton Combe Junior School, near Bath, during the 1940s from a well-known independent school affected by the threat of German raids. To Michael he was simply known as 'Mr Inchley' (later acquiring the names 'Skipper', 'JI' and 'Commy'). He was young and active, seeking to know the boys better. Besides his teaching he was a rugby ('rugger') coach of enthusiasm if not great skill, and more importantly he was the Scoutmaster.

'We became excited at the talk of a Scout camp being restarted,' Michael writes. 'In war time, of course, they were hard to run, so one day when Mr Inchley told us we were going to the South Somerset Quantocks we were thrilled.

'With our bags packed about four of us settled into the open back of a lorry heading for the Quantocks, so far unknown at all to us. We were very excited and as the hedges got nearer we would snatch at the branches. One lad painfully snatched a briar branch!

'I don't know how you know Great Wood now, but you must try to imagine our journey. We came to the edge of the hills. Then we came into an opening surrounded by hundreds of smaller newly grown fir trees clustered together. My first reaction was to wonder what creatures lived in their close dark shade. In those days the track was almost level with the field, but it has subsequently been built up.

'We went into the field and of course very soon discovered the stream on the far side, one of Great Wood's greatest attractions over all the years. Both banks are in quite close contact and nowhere is it too deep, nor too shallow to create dams and bridges and such like. It is not muddy or rocky. A perfect camp stream and one from which a pool could later be created.

'When the main party arrived next day we soon had the patrol tents up, and a slightly larger main tent for a gathering space and stores. This was established in the southern corner near where cabins 5 and 6 would be built.

'In the days ahead we used the forest and the hills for exploring and "wide games". One group got lost coming back from a hike that had taken them to the coast!

'The whole atmosphere had to be experienced, as indeed it still does today with all its changes. The evenings were perfect times of relaxing together, with singing and talks of the Christian faith so dear to Commy and his fellow helpers.

'It is no surprise that Great Wood has so established itself over the years.

But the journey was to take another twist.

My [John Inchley's] *teaching days were coming to an end and I was to be invited to join the staff of Children's Special Service Mission as a children's evangelist. A second camp, however, was held on the Quantocks site in 1944 under the CSSM banner. It was still under canvas and provided scope for Scouting activities. The site was proving itself to be more and more attractive, and a spring holiday camp was held in the following school Easter holidays using the Women's Institute Hall for greater security from the weather. This was situated in the village of Over Stowey in the hamlet of Adscombe; it was also called the Campbell Rooms and was near enough to the camping field on which three tents were pitched.*

Opposite to the Women's Institute was sited a wartime Nissen hut already vacated, and handed over to the farmer on whose land it stood. The Nissen hut gave rise to the idea of establishing a permanent camp, and with this in mind, the farmer, who now owned the hut, was tentatively approached. He was willing to sell but was asking rather a high price.

In the autumn of 1945, the same year in which the spring camp was held in the Campbell Rooms, it so happened that, while visiting in the area of the Quantocks, I was prompted to pay a second visit to the owner of the Nissen hut. The farmer was free and only too ready to show his caller round the building. Although, as I thought, there was no money available as yet, I felt strangely and suddenly compelled to agree to the lower figure the farmer was now asking and entered into an agreement of purchase there and then. What I did not know at the time, of course, was that there was a most generous cheque already in the post from a wealthy friend with whom the project had been shared, and that this would completely meet the purchase price which had been agreed with the farmer. Interestingly enough this donation of £60 was the largest gift received at that time and was a very real indication to everyone concerned of the wonderful provision which was to be made by a loving Heavenly Father for the total establishment of the camp. At the same time, however, an appeal was being made to contribute towards the cost of creating the permanent camp as a thanksgiving for the continuation during the war years of the boys' normal holiday activities. Nearly £300 was donated by fifty-seven subscribers, which was a considerable amount of money in the 1940s. So the Nissen hut was purchased for £60, although it cost £240 for removal and re-erection including the concrete floor for its base.

Mr Tucker had already been approached and it was discovered that he was agreeable for the camping field to become a permanency at a reasonable rent with a ten-year lease and an opportunity eventually to purchase nearly five acres of freehold land for the very attractive sum of £300. Mr Tucker, in the early days, very generously provided free storage in one of his barns for various items of camping equipment until they could be safely accommodated on the campsite. Subsequently, when he sold his farm five or six years later to Mr Ben Bartlett, the camping field was left out of the sale and purchased by Scripture Union in whom the whole project was vested. Incidentally Mr Bartlett with his wife and family, like the Tuckers before them, became very good friends, and when some extra useful land became available they readily sold it to the camp.

Much still had to be done. Planning permission for the erection of the buildings was obtained. The Nissen hut was removed from Mr Tom Biffen's land and re-erected on the camping field by a Bridgwater builder. The project had to be properly legalised, which was carried out by Scripture Union Camping Headquarters. The Nissen hut needed furnishing while the task of providing sleeping quarters for campers and helpers had to be addressed.

Watercolour by PG Scott of the Nissen hut

The Chapel

The secluded area of the open-air camp chapel had been cleared of its undergrowth during the early days of the Great Wood project. The clearing thus made was large enough to accommodate a hundred persons, and benches were carried from the mess hut on occasional Sundays in the right kind of weather in order that services might be held. The only drawback was that the iron legs of the benches were apt to sink into the ground, which was chaotic for the occupants. But the chapel was a most idyllic place and just right for worshipping God. Situated at the top end of the field, and completely hidden from sight by a mass of wild rhododendron, it was full of animation. The stream formed its far boundary with its constant chatter everlastingly and musically breaking the silence. On the near side, in front of the rhododendron, was a ditch over which a bridge was built which, together with a wrought iron gate, provided a narrow and inconspicuous entrance. The clearing was encircled by a variety of deciduous trees with their branches forming a natural and cathedral-like canopy overhead, and the accumulation of their fallen leaves during the autumns of countless years producing a soft and substantial mattress to walk upon beneath.

The First Buildings

After much searching, and appeals to the War Department in Bristol for the provision of surplus buildings, it was discovered in a seemingly roundabout way that there was a quantity of wooden cabins stockpiled somewhere in Wiltshire. They were earmarked for another purpose but it was agreed, after a deal of wrangling, that I should be allowed to purchase twelve of them at £7.50 each (£7.10s in those days).

A trunk call was put through to London and Scripture Union Camps Department agreed to make a loan (since refunded in full) for their immediate purchase. The cabins in sections were eventually delivered and ten of them were promptly erected on the camping field in a half-circle by a retired local builder named Ware of Aley, another hamlet of Over Stowey. The staff of Rubery Owen of Darlaston most generously donated a sufficient number of two-tier and three-tier bunks complete with mattresses; additional mattresses were purchased which meant that

Original cabin with Vardo in distance

the sleeping needs of everyone were fully met. The erected cabins were numbered 1 to 10. Number 10 was still standing in 1988, though it had a new roof which was provided in 1953; numbers 1 and 2 were also re-roofed and joined together in 1953; subsequently they became sleeping quarters for helpers and were called 'Old Number 1', which name has stuck. The final two of the wooden cabins were, later on, erected as a latrine hut. They have been replaced since that time with a more suitable building.

The Nissen hut was divided into a mess hut and kitchen with a serving hatch in between. The kitchen was provided with a very efficient solid fuel stove and an equally useful paraffin oil cooker. Later on the solid fuel stove was replaced by an Esse cooker from the Over Stowey vicarage which, in turn, together with the paraffin stove, gave way to Calor Gas cookers, a Calor Gas hot plate, and a water boiler for tea and other hot drinks. (Originally a massive Primus was placed under a standard water boiler for this purpose.)

Tables and Forms

The fact remained that the meals section of the Nissen hut was still without tables and chairs. This was remedied by the acquisition of both of these in what was generally felt were truly remarkable ways. The tables were acquired first of all. It happened at an auction sale of surplus wartime materials in Bath. One of the unexpected lots was at least sixteen well-made six-foot-long wartime bunks which I reckoned could be made into tables, once they were altered. So, very prayerfully, when the lot came to be auctioned, I bid for them and they were knocked down to me for very much less than new tables would have cost, had they been obtainable at the end of the war; new tables in any case would have been of inferior quality. The purchased bunks had very strong plywood tops with rows of circular holes an inch or so in diameter apparently for the purpose of ventilation of the wartime beds. The plywood was eventually stripped off half of the bunks and re-nailed to the square reverse side, thus making eight or so table tops. The plywood was also stripped off the remainder, producing the requisite number of frames for legs. These frames had well-made strengthening bars, which, when slightly shortened, made ideal pairs of legs which were hinged to the table tops at each end, and made rigid when in use by easily manipulated iron bars. This meant that the tables were collapsible and could be stacked, which was a necessity when extra space was needed for meetings or other activities. All of this work was undertaken quite freely by a Monkton Combe builder parent in Bath whose children came to the camp in the early days. He very kindly arranged for the work to be carried out in one of his workshops and also stored the finished tables until they were needed. The original bunks were very well made and provided most excellent tables which were still in use thirty years afterwards. Subsequently, because the spillage of food soaking into the plywood tops produced a sour smell, and also because upset liquids ran through the ventilation holes on to the knees of the campers and helpers, the tables were covered with brown battleship linoleum. This also had the effect of considerably enhancing their appearance.

'Over the years,' says Bill Carter, camper and leader from 1967, 'the original tables have been replaced firstly by much heavier, less robust stackable ones and more recently by some lighter ones with fixed legs. Neither design has been as durable or as versatile. We wait with eager anticipation to see how the next table design compares!'

If the production of the tables was quite wonderful the provision of the benches was even more so. But it followed a long chapter of accidents which, however, ended happily enough and to the advantage of the camp. The benches, like the tables, were surplus wartime items, but came from a factory in Birmingham. Once again the quality was good, and the benches were stackable – a very important feature. There seemed to be hundreds of benches at the factory though some were the worse for wear through being stacked out-of-doors; as a result the metal of their legs had become rusty. It was most definitely stipulated, therefore, that the ones to be supplied must come from the indoor stock, and this was agreed. When the benches arrived, however, they all had rusty legs and had obviously come from the out-of-doors batch. The Christian representative at the factory was full of apologies when he was informed of the discrepancy and promised to make arrangements for them to be replaced. Then a message was received that the poor-quality benches had been despatched a second time while the selected ones were to follow immediately. The conclusion of all this was that the camp found itself with forty-eight or so benches, only a third of which were usable in the mess hut. The cost of returning them would have been prohibitive, so an intrepid but reasonable offer was made for the lot, and willingly accepted. The satisfactory result was that the complete consignment cost no more than the very attractive price agreed for the original quantity. The good benches were duly used in the Nissen hut while a number of the poorer ones were shortened to provide the cabins with useful out-of-doors seating … these shortened benches were easily carried across the field and supplied necessary forms when there was a camp fire. The wood from the remainder, a commodity which was at a premium in the years immediately following the war, was employed in all kinds of useful ways around the camp.

Receptacles

At the early camps those who attended were instructed to bring their own receptacles and knives and forks while the camp supplied the necessary bowls and jugs and serving dishes, which were purchased at an attractive price from a Christian firm of suppliers at St Albans. Later on the camp provided all the items which the campers and helpers were originally directed to bring with them. Much later on the camp replaced the Pyrex dishes and the earthenware jugs with stainless steel units which not only improved the appearance of the tables when they were laid for meals but were unbreakable if dropped.

The Workers

So it came about that the first permanent Christian camp was to be just ready for occupation during the school holidays of Easter 1946 when a small group of boys would be welcomed. This was to be preceded by a 'working party', a tradition which has continued over the Easter bank holiday ever since. The willing helpers who formed this working party painted the outside of the Nissen hut, bolted together the three-tier bunks, and did all sorts of other things, as they generally prepared for the future camps which it was hoped would take place in the months and years to come.

This meant that not only were all the material necessities provided but, from the very beginning, there was a group of dedicated men and women who were not only ready to give themselves to the needs and activities of the camp but who had also caught the vision of its potential. The only exceptions were unavoidable, and mostly consisted of university students who, by force of their commitments, were unable to tie themselves to anything lasting; there was also a man named Vine Martin from far-away New Zealand, who had to return; he was at the very first working party camp and did a great job of work.

The Motivation

The fact is that no one ever sat down and thought up the establishment of a permanent camp. It just seemed to happen, while those who were responsible for its construction were simply endeavouring to be faithful stewards and to do what they believed they were being told to do. They were also intrepid enough to presume that all they were doing was by the motivation of God himself. They are anxious to give God the glory for all that took place.

Of course the camp needed a name. Perhaps the conception of this had been subconsciously formed in my mind when, as far back as 1938, a brochure was received at the school where I was teaching giving details of a secular permanent camp which had been established for school boys in the Thames Valley. It was actually called 'Big Wood Camp'! Could it possibly savour of plagiarism if the new camp in the Quantocks was called 'Great Wood'? An alternative was 'Seven Wells Camp' after the combe in which it was situated. But not only did it not sound as befitting; it was felt that such a name might forebode dampness to anxious parents! The Ordnance map designation for the forest on the eastern side of the camp was 'Great Wood'. Eventually, therefore, it was decided to risk the possible suggestion of plagiarism and use the title 'Great Wood Camp'. This title has remained and has become very precious to a countless number of individuals over the years. It is now marked as 'Great Wood Camp' on the Ordnance Survey maps.

Perhaps the most important requirement is water. The water in the stream itself was pure enough, though it was realised that a dead animal's carcase might be rotting away somewhere in its upper reaches as it meandered through the forest undergrowth. Water for cooking and drinking, therefore, was obtained from one of the numerous springs that seemed to abound at the top end of the camping field. It was here at the back of Cabin 10 that a simple well was dug in the earliest days of the permanent camp. The well was made just large enough to house a small galvanised tank which the nearby spring easily and quickly filled and into which clean buckets, kept especially for the purpose, could be dipped. These water-filled buckets were then carried, two at a time, on an old-fashioned yoke, by an odd jobs man who emptied their contents into the tank outside the kitchen door. The cooks, however, seemed to use a tremendous amount of water and there was a constant cry for the tank's replenishment. The well was dug in 1946 and was most successful, but in 1949 the unsatisfactory and burdensome carrying of water was to be brought to a welcome end. It had lasted three long years.

11

The end was dependent on iron piping which was in short supply and very precious at that time. It was discovered, however, that Sir Alfred Owen, the Christian chairman of Rubery Owen of Darlaston, and a parent friend of the camp, was able and willing to supply the necessary lengths. These were needed so that there might be a gravity flow from the well to a large tank that was to be buried in the ground at the kitchen end of the Nissen hut. A similar tank was to be fixed to the roof of the Nissen into which the piped water was to be pumped by hand from below. This meant that there could be running water with taps over the kitchen sink. A paraffin-fired hot water boiler was later installed so that there could always be a plentiful supply of both hot and cold water so long as the tank on the roof was kept full. Every camper, helpers as well as boys and girls, was supposed to do just over thirty hand pumps a day in order to achieve this. The hot and cold water was also a great boon to the washers-up. The cooks, however, still ran short and a cry would often be made from the precincts of the kitchen for more water to be pumped.

Swimming Pools

The first pool was built around 1947. Before that the stream was suitably dammed and where the water was deepened as a result of this the campers used to splash about. It seems that it was all that they could do. The first swimming pool was not much better; it was very small but had the advantage that it was deep enough to swim, though it did not have a sufficient depth of water for diving. Photographs show that it was very small indeed; not longer, in fact, than approximately ten feet or long enough for seven campers to sit side by side on its longest edge in order to splash with their feet. The width of the pool was proportional to the length. It was also built with makeshift corrugated iron sheets for shuttering, leaving corrugations in the concrete of the finished pool. Unfortunately it leaked slightly so that water from the stream had constantly to be allowed to run into it, which caused it to be cold at all times. It was malignantly, though light-heartedly, called the mud bath by the campers! However, it was better than nothing.

First Campers

Brian was John Inchley's stepson and was one of the first campers. His sisters Carol (five years old) and Rosemary (four months old) went in 1944. Carol recalls Rosemary being bathed in a papier-mâché bath outside their tent. It was to become their second home as most of their Easter and summer holidays were spent at Great Wood.

1950s: Girls Arrive

The girls' camps began as early as 1951, and at the beginning, for a number of years, were efficiently led by Mrs Archibald, affectionately known as Tim [or 'Mrs A']. Her husband, Roddy Archibald, always attended these camps until he died, and was justly remembered for his great work in India with the Children's Special Service Mission. Mrs Archibald, at the girls' camps, had the stalwart help of Mrs Lechler, who had been a Guide captain, and so was all ready to take advantage of all that Great Wood so abundantly provided.

Jane Sutton also recalls those early girls' camps. Mrs Elizabeth Archibald reigned supreme as the commandant. Jane was an officer under her on several occasions. Roddy would stay in the farmhouse at the beginning of the Combe. It was Jane's duty each morning to go to the farmhouse, collect the mail and return with Roddy to the camp for the day. It was an enormous privilege to talk with him on those walks.

'Because of the India connection, we always had to have a curry during the course of the camp. *But* ... it had to be cooked properly; no hastily put together concoction! It was prepared the evening before and allowed to mature overnight – and, needless to say, it was very tasty.

'The Archibalds had a large, detailed and accurate model of the Tabernacle, similar to Hudson Pope's version. At one camp, it was laid out in the mess hut and we had wonderful and very memorable talks on each of the parts and furnishings. The symbolism was mesmerising. But all Mrs A's talks were good and there were always plenty of homemade visual aids; no videos or PowerPoint in those days.

'Many of us look back with affection and gratitude to those

camps. Our officers would arrive a day early to prepare, while the boys' camp officers were clearing up. This meant that we also got to know JI and his wife and children. I was in my early twenties then.'

JI continues:

There were also mixed camps. These took place mostly at Whitsuntide for boys and girls, ages eight to eleven, from the churches where I had held children's missions. Older children, on the other hand, ages fourteen upwards, gladly came to the spartan camps held during the Easter school holidays. These camps were originally led by myself and Mrs Inchley with a good team of helpers, as were the Whitsuntide camps. With the helpers, I introduced all kinds of novel activities to the Easter camps, including drama and country dancing, with a view to meeting the needs of those who attended. Prayers were always lively sessions when teenage problems were valiantly faced.

Camps in the early days were very military, at least in the titles that they gave to their helpers, and Great Wood was no exception to this. The leader of the camp was always known as the commandant, supported by his adjutant. The helper who ordered the food and arranged the meals was known as the quartermaster, while he had various assistants, one of whom was in charge of the campers on duty, who were called orderlies. The quartermaster's associates were given the title of sub-quartermaster. The ordinary helpers were called officers and in the earliest days were always addressed as Mister so-and-so. But it was certainly untrue that the camps at Great Wood were at all military in character, and this was shown by the manner that the high sounding titles were always contracted. The commandant was consistently known as Commy, while his adjutant was renamed Adjy. The quartermaster was reduced in title to Quarters or QM, while his helpers were known as subbies.

The leader of the camp also had the responsibility given to him by Camp Headquarters of training the other helpers, and certainly at Great Wood he did his best. He organised prayer meetings and Bible studies and also felt it was his duty to train in the less spiritual activities of the camp.

There was a tradition at Great Wood amongst the helpers of 'feet washing' with regard to the boys and girls (see John 13:3–15). This meant that no camper should have an unsolved problem, such as having lost something, which the helper did not help him to disentangle. Usually the term was metaphorical though sometimes there needed to be a physical washing of children's tired feet after a strenuous hike on the hills. I remember that one day in the camp surgery I gave a boy, with blisters on his feet, a bowl of potassium permanganate solution in which to soak his feet. Then I was called away, and forgot my patient for more than half an hour. Boy-like, the camper was still there when I returned, his feet in the bowl becoming more and more deeply stained with the liquid which can be used for staining floors as well as dealing with tender feet. With horror and dismay I found myself wondering if the feet would ever return to their natural colour, and dreading having to return the boy to his fond parents with his extremities stained a vivid purple!

The campers were trained, too, not only to put Jesus first in their lives and to continue this by daily reading of the Bible and prayer at home, but also how to fight the good fight and be victorious. The older campers were also taught the value of tithing. The camp motto for everyone was 'Endure Hardness', while all the camp activities were directed towards this (see King James version of 2 Timothy 2:3). There was never to be the slightest semblance of ragging of helpers, or bullying of less attractive campers, or any other form of horse-play which so often occurs when children are left on their own with insufficient activity to engage their lively minds. There was, however, plenty of fun in the camps at Great Wood.

Early Commandants

Horace Webber was commandant of an extra boys' camp in 1956, and had the good and efficient Brian Stanley for his adjutant. Horace continued to lead these camps for a number of years until he was forced to discontinue because of ill health. He had Trevor Briant as adjutant in the latter years. But Horace played a very enterprising part in all the activities of Great Wood, and was camp secretary for fifteen years. He also regularly saw off the London campers from Paddington station.

Another stalwart of the early camps was Commy Roberts. He was the founder and headmaster of Brocksford Hall, a boys' preparatory school in Derbyshire from which a large number of boys revelled in the delight of

Great Wood in the early days. Commy Roberts was a Broads expert and a commandant in his own right.

Mention must also be made of Howard Heeley, who was originally John Roberts' right-hand man when the school was at Sheffield. Howard, during the war years, became headmaster of Birkdale, the original school in Sheffield from which he regularly brought a number of his boys to the camp. Howard was a real character, driving his antiquated car to Taunton at the beginning of the camp, putting it into a garage, and returning to Sheffield by train in order that he might personally supervise his boys' journey. He followed the same procedure in reverse on the return trip. Many are the stories that can be told of this remarkable man. For example, he was perhaps the only one who could conduct morning prayers and answer the telephone to a parent, both at the same time!

David Gardiner was my adjutant at most of the camps in the early days and was wholeheartedly involved in the project of establishing a permanent camp. He was a man of many parts and a real countryman. I still remember the trout that David caught from the stream in the early mornings and himself cooked most expertly for an addition to the Commy's breakfast. They were delicious in the extreme! David played the small harmonium too (popularly called the Pandemonium), while another of my vivid memories is of David's bare feet as he tirelessly pumped the instrument with great vigour in order to bring out the best sound. He was not beyond repairing the harmonium either when it was called for. In latter days there was a piano by courtesy of Monkton Combe School and Mr Kenneth Guy.

Cooks

No camp can function without food and the lady cooks who came regularly to Great Wood were indispensable. Dilys Gething was at the camps from almost the very beginning and learnt to cook out-of-doors for one of the summer camps, something which was not covered by the domestic science college that she was attending. But she was a most excellent and adaptable cook. She was joined by Mary Gladstone in 1947. Mary had cooked at earlier camps run by myself and my wife in North Wales in 1945 and 1946. She came to Great Wood every year until 1961 ... she missed for family reasons in 1962 and 1963 but was back again from 1964 to 1968.

17

She was a Cambridge graduate, a Cambridge Blue and a highly respected editor in a Christian publishing house. Both Dilys and Mary were outstanding Christians. Dilys, later in life, was an important helper of David Sheppard at the Mayflower Centre.

Mary Gladstone, cook from 1947 until 1968, recalls the 'old shepherd' getting up at about 5am to light the fire in the Mrs Sam cooker so that it was hot enough for putting on the dixie of porridge at 7am. Stirring the porridge first thing in the morning was a very hot job. Milk was collected from Bartlett's farm in churns until the early seventies and stored in the stream to keep it cool. The butter would be in a dixie in the stream.

Rationing was still in place when Mary initially went to camp and JI was very particular about each boy getting his four ounces of meat when carving the Sunday roast, a tradition carried on into the 1970s.

Carving the Sunday roast

The plates also had to be warmed, Mary remembers, and this was done using a paraffin plate warmer. On one occasion the wick must have been too long and the plates, when fetched out, were covered in black soot which took quite a lot of washing off. Mugs could only be two-thirds filled to prevent spillage on the tables. Plates all had the VPS (Varsity and Public Schools Camps) logo on them, and woe betide you if this wasn't always placed at twelve o'clock; laying tables correctly was considered very important.

JI vividly remembered Janet Hood, another cook.

[Janet] *was a Scot and had a habit of calling a spade a spade. She said to me one day, probably after a mild altercation in the kitchen, 'You need not think that it is you we come for, it is Mrs I.' Janet sadly died in her early years. Another cook who died young was Faith Rayner: they both were truly wonderful Christians.*

Lynette Weekley came and cooked for a number of years. She was not only an accomplished teacher but became an advanced car driver; she was also a quite wonderful skier. In fact she was skiing officer to the older girls who attended the mixed winter sports camp that I and Mrs Inchley led during the Christmas holidays.

There were other ladies too, notably Rosemary Lund, who was also a prominent schoolteacher and spoke French fluently. It was she who commenced the tradition at the campers' swell dinner that the lady cooks' speech should be given in French. It was detrimentally and shockingly discovered, however, that the words of one of her speeches mostly came from the label on a sauce bottle! But it did not matter very much for most of the campers and helpers failed to understand a single word she uttered, though they all enjoyed the speech immensely. Rosemary eventually was married by me to David Gardiner and they have been extremely happy together, God having given them two splendid boys.

The Vardo

This story would certainly be incomplete without some mention of the Vardo or Romany caravan. This was presented to me as a personal gift in 1953 from the helpers and campers at Great Wood in order to mark

19

my twenty-five years of leading camps for children. The caravan was seemingly purchased from a site near Bournemouth, provided with new wheels, painted grey, and delivered to the camp on a low-loader lorry. I was delighted with the gift – it was just what I had dreamed of and I valued this magnificent gift most highly. I also valued the small brass plate bearing the telling words, 'THOUGH ABSENT YET WITH YOU IN THE SPIRIT', which is a happy reminder of the first part of verse 5 in Colossians chapter 2.

The caravan, solidly made of wood, had concrete blocks made to prevent its four beautiful wheels from resting on the ground, and was soon painted on the outside with bright variegated colours. Inside, the antiquated stove and chimney were removed, and the brass plate and VPSC crest fastened to the walls. Altogether the interior of the van was made very much more homely. The bed, turned into a long seat during the day, was very comfortable, and I used it for sleeping when my daughters, as well as my wife, were resident in the camp. Previously I had used Cabin No. 1 for my headquarters, and the arrival of the Romany caravan just as the original campers' cabins were being enlarged and refurbished meant that Cabin No. 1 would as we have seen be utilised for these significant enlargements.

The Vardo did good service for nineteen years until I left Great Wood in 1971. Folk came especially to the camp to gaze at it, while campers were intrigued by its bright colours. It was a popular place for photographs. However, quite apart from the fact that it was a personal gift, it was realised that the van would need a large amount of maintenance so, very reluctantly, it was advertised and eventually sold.

Letting to Christian Groups

The site was also let to other Christian groups. These included parties of boys from West of England Crusader classes who visited the camp on a number of occasions, a party of boys from Scotland and boys from Kingham Hill School in Oxfordshire and Mr Graham Oliver's Lifeboys from Morden in Outer London.

Probably the most unconventional of these lettings, which I always enjoyed when I was present, was to the London Lifeboys. This was possibly due to the precise leadership of Graham Oliver himself, who was not only a positive disciplinarian, but also a most meticulous time-keeper. His Lifeboys came as often as they were able from 1953 onwards, and were always fully occupied.

Mr Oliver, as well as possessing a Rolls Bentley car, also owned a Land Rover and a most robust trailer which was brought to the camp, fully loaded with stores and equipment, by a senior helper. Noel Carpenter, another of Graham's senior helpers, also owned a Land Rover with an equally robust trailer which he brought to the camp as well. They both, from time to time, filled these trailers with boys who, in order to provide sufficient room, were ordered to stand. The purpose of all this was to transport the campers to distant parts of the forest. This was probably strictly against the law, but was nevertheless thoroughly successful, while the boys' enjoyment of the experience was most marked.

These lettings of the camp, as did all the tenancies, brought in some money but were also, hopefully, greatly beneficial to the thousands of children who occupied Great Wood and who, by and large, appreciated the amenities which were provided.

Letting to the Local Education Authority

The most long-standing of the other lettings was to the Local Education Authority, which all began in the early days of the project with a committed Christian named Frank Dain who held an important PE job with the administration. The tradition has been ably continued with Tom Elkin and Derek Briggs – Derek puts the number of children who have benefited from the good things provided by Great Wood not at thousands, but at tens of thousands. The present appointment by the Authority is definitely worthy of the succession, namely one Cate Sampson who, besides playing hockey for Somerset Ladies, is a very real supporter of the general aims of the camp.

The LEA is also the longest, duration-wise, of the users of the camp as it brings mostly junior school children to Great Wood, a week at a time, for the whole of the Easter term and a part of the Christmas term when Scripture Union is not using the place. The camp never loses its popularity.

The Camper Who Was Left Behind

Only once, and this by one of the tenancy lettings, was a boy left behind at Great Wood while his fellow campers were taken to be collected, at a far distant rendezvous, by their fond parents who would personally convey them to their several homes. It was partly the boy's own fault. His parents had visited the camp while on holiday in the neighbourhood and their son mistakenly had thought they had said that they would be collecting him from Great Wood on the day the camp ended. He was quite sure about this when questioned, so much so that he refused to go with the other boys when they left promptly in the mid-morning, partly in a coach and partly in the camp leader's car. So this forlorn youngster was left behind in the charge of a senior helper who still had a number of chores to complete in order that the camp could be handed over in a spick and span condition. Later in the morning of the same day this helper offered to take the boy home in his car as they both lived in the same district. The boy, who was feeling more and more miserable when his parents failed to materialise and was also, apparently, having second thoughts about the entire business, gladly accepted the generous offer. Meanwhile the camp leader had arrived at the named meeting spot where his boys were to be collected, only to be greeted by the angry father of the boy who had been left behind. The father had actually thought for his part that he had told his son that he would collect him at the specified meeting place and not at the camp at all. The camp leader was all for returning to Great Wood there and then but the father insisted on making the long journey himself. But when he reached the camp in West Somerset at last, he found, of course, that his offspring had already left, and was angrier than ever, as well he might be. Apparently, he spent a full fortnight nursing his bitterness, when at last he reached home, before he was able to calm down sufficiently to forget the whole escapade. He also, eventually, had the grace to apologise to the leader of the camp, while readily accepting the blame for the happening through not being sufficiently explicit to his son as to the exact place where he would collect him.

Family Memories

Rosemary Watson, JI's daughter, recalls that 'I must have been about ten years old, old enough to be allowed to sit in on the evening talks. I had said "yes" to Jesus, aged seven, at home, my dad praying with me. He wrote in a copy of John Stott's *Your Confirmation*, and then gave it to me eight years later when I was confirmed. The evening talk found me in tears; I wanted to respond to my father's invitation to the campers to say "yes" to Jesus. But I'd already done so. My dad came to the rescue of my tears and explained that growing up was about saying a bigger "yes" to God. And that's what I've been doing ever since.

'As I became a teenager and joined in the Youth Focus activities, it became my turn and privilege as a cabin leader to engage with younger people in deepening their response to the implications of handing over their autonomy to God.

'And so it has gone on! Thank you, Lord (and thank you, Great Wood and my dad!).'

Water

The improved water supply installed in 1949 was a good one and lasted for six years until, in 1955, the manual activity was replaced by a petrol pump with a two-stroke engine. Once it was started this was most efficient though the motor was temperamental from time to time, usually because the sparking plug was dirty, or the supply of petrol had run out. The cooks, therefore, still ran short of water and had to call for a fresh supply.

The petrol pump was also extremely noisy and one eventful day two years later ... I was endeavouring to rest with the sound of the motor running during a siesta break at the end of a series of camps when, lo and behold, I was given the breath-taking notion of tapping the stream high enough in the combe, through which the stream flowed, to provide a gravity flow of water, at least for cooking and washing up, with the consequence of eliminating the bulk of pumping altogether. I could not help wondering why I had not thought of it sooner. While it was certainly a hare-brained idea it was compulsive enough for a letter to be written and posted to the Forestry Commission in Bristol, whose permission and co-operation would be necessary if such a preposterous scheme was to materialise. For a long time there was no reply and I had almost given up altogether. Then, one day, in the grocery-store-cum-post-office at Nether Stowey, which was the nearest shopping village to Great Wood, I was button-holed by the local head forester, who happened to be there at the same time. Yes, the letter had been received, and did the camp leader know that there was a well above the camp? Certainly not!

There and then an agreement was made for a meeting, when the man-made well was revealed. It was hidden away by the forest undergrowth and even now cannot be easily discovered. It is just a rough catchment of stones for a stream of the purest water endlessly flowing from the side of the hills, and probably made many years previously and forgotten. Readers of this story may judge the excitement this produced! Should the water in the catchment area be high enough it would flow by gravity and fill the roof-top tank and the noisy and painstaking pumping would be brought to an end. During the winter following, the levels were professionally surveyed in bitterly cold weather and it was realistically and wonderfully discovered that the water from the catchment was just high enough to flow by gravity into the tank on the roof. In point of fact a really strong wooden tower was newly built instead with an up-to-date container holding 250 gallons placed on its summit, after an agreement for the use of the supply had been entered into with the Forestry Commission for only a peppercorn rental. Plastic piping, which had the property of being burst-proof in freezing weather, was laid from the spring in the woods to the new tank, while the joy of everyone concerned can scarcely be imagined when the first rush of water began to flow without any pumping at all into the tank on top of the tower. Although it did not take place until 1958, fourteen years after the establishment of the permanent camp, it was an obvious illustration of the Water of Life. The catchment area with its overflowing spring had been there all the time when the water to supply the evident needs of the campers was being carried in buckets, and piped and pumped, first of all by hand and then by a noisy temperamental pump. It was there all the time when the cooks were calling for fresh supplies. But everyone was in complete ignorance of its existence, and that it was just waiting to be used.

There is no doubt that in this connection we should remember the words of the Lord Jesus recorded in John 7:37, 'If a man is thirsty let him come to me and drink.' We will also want to recall the well-known lines of Horatius Bonar's hymn,

I heard the voice of Jesus say,
'Behold I freely give
The living water – thirsty one,
Stoop down and drink and live.'
I came to Jesus and I drank
Of that life giving stream.
My thirst was quenched, my soul revived,
And now I live in Him.

But so many, in our day and age, are simply ignorant of these important and necessary things. The spring, which now supplies Great Wood with the purest of water, has never once abated for thirty years even in the driest of summers. It must be admitted, however, that the original installation was not quite perfect. Occasionally, especially in the earliest days, there were air locks simply because the levels were critical. But this problem was overcome with comparative ease. Nowadays the catchment source is still being used, while, with the coming of the electricity, the water is pumped automatically around the camp.

A Different Way of Life

John Langford, camper and team from 1952, recalls, 'John and Mary Inchley visited my parents in Hereford in the summer of 1952, and I came to the last camp at Great Wood of that summer in late August. My memory is that camps lasted longer in those times – twelve days, to be precise.

'The cabins in those days were less than half the size of the present cabins, housing five or six boys each. In the halo doubles tournament, I was paired with Stephen Houghton (nephew of the hymn-writing Bishop Houghton) and he was marvellously agile.

25

He patrolled the back of the court fielding the many opportunities which I missed at the front, and we eventually emerged the winners (almost certainly the only occasion on which I've won any game played on a court). Stephen sadly was later murdered at Marsabit in northern Kenya, where he was working as a missionary.

'John Inchley was wonderfully lucid in his talks at the end of each day. As well as walks on Exmoor, we had a memorable visit to the large open-air swimming pool at Minehead, where bold lads (not from our party) would sit on each other's shoulders and dive in together from a great height off the diving stand. Health and safety seemed less emphasised sixty-five years ago!

'On September 8th, the day before camp ended, the Exmoor Staghounds came baying past the campsite on the far side of the field in full pursuit of a stag, which must have been in the last extremity of exhaustion. It was cornered by the buildings of Adscombe Farm and shot by the huntsman, who then drew his knife and slit it straight along its underside before feeding its steaming entrails to the hungry hounds. One of the slots (hooves) was given to John Inchley, who had it mounted and hung on the wall of the mess hut (which is how I know the exact date).'

Sanitation

As late as 1952 or 1953 two cabins were erected side by side in order to form a fresh sanitary block. This was originally euphemistically called the North West until it was renamed Adam and Eve, whenever there was a camp catering for both sexes. It was a great improvement on the original one which must have been open to the weather. The new sanitary block also had two cold taps and could be divided by a strong lockable door when there was a mixed camp. It had Elsan chemical closets while a concrete tank was constructed at the rear for their discharge.

The existence of unlimited water from 1958 onwards meant, among other things, that the old Elsan chemical closets could give way to the more modern flushing type and that these could be installed in the same

The first Adam and Eve

building. But this was not without unexpected difficulties. First of all there was the difficulty of the Camps Committee in London where one member was actually reported as saying that the innovation would rob the camp of some of its atmosphere. This member could not have spoken a truer word, for the partly full Elsan containers had to be emptied into the tank at the rear of the sanitary block and the containers recharged with the Elsan chemical fluid which was brown and sticky, very different from the more modern type. It was a messy and strong-smelling business, and was undertaken in the early morning, before the campers were up, only by the leaders of the camp or very trusted senior helpers. Certainly the 'atmosphere' was anything but pleasant and the loss of it mentioned by the Camps Committee member in London was by no means to be lamented. Arrangements had also to be made with a firm named Harris regularly to empty the concrete tank into which the Elsan closets were emptied. After one particularly wet winter this tank sprang a leak and would constantly fill with water. The firm of Harris was contacted at their local branch in Bridgwater. They dealt with the emergency and were successful in emptying the tank, but instead of discharging the effluent in the usual place they released it somewhere at the head of the combe where it slightly fouled the drinking water. It is not remembered what happened next, but the fouling was very temporary, while the leak in the concrete tank was soon repaired.

The second problem had to do with the satisfactory installation of a septic tank because there was no mains sewage available. It was decided that the site was near to the stream below the camp where the overflow, which was supposed to be drinkable, could flow into the swiftly running water. The septic tank had to be according to the local council's specifications and was eventually passed by them as satisfactory. Since then it has been doubled in size. But, by the time that these problems and other minor ones had all been overcome the new water closets were not in use until 1962 or 1963.

Four flushing toilets with all their component parts were generously provided by a parent builder named Mr Charles Rose of Nottingham. They were delivered by his now grown-up son in a Land Rover with a message that they were to constitute an Easter offering seeing that I no longer had a parish!

Banda Hut

The Banda hut was erected in 1958. A piece of land at the far end of the camping field near to the swimming pool had become vacant. It was previously used by one of the residents in Adscombe for keeping poultry and pigs – a fact which had some drawbacks for the camp. If the land could be purchased it would also square up the camp field. The land now belonged to Farmer Bartlett who, on being approached, agreed to sell.

The land in question was situated behind a tall hedge which was cut down to a more modest height in order to preserve a semblance of privacy. A gate was fixed for a way through, and a sizeable hut was erected on the site. The hut, from the beginning, had a partition inside, with a door, beyond which was a small kitchen and a place for washing. The hut also had outside doors at the front and on the kitchen side. It had a big window facing the camp. At the beginning there were no drains and any surplus water had to be thrown into the hedge. The original chemical closet at the rear of the building was replaced some years later by a proper lavatory connected satisfactorily to the septic tank sited nearby. The Banda hut was lit originally by Calor Gas changed most successfully later on for electricity.

Inside, the hut was very bare at first, but a most generous gift of cedar wood for its lining was made by a prominent Christian timber merchant named Graham Oliver who was a great friend of the camp. This had a most pleasing scent, and made a tremendous difference to the interior of the hut both aesthetically and practically. The only drawback was what seemed like thousands of house flies which chose to hibernate behind the panelling and would come out again for a very short span of life as soon as the hut warmed in the spring. These dead flies were gathered up in their multitudes and summarily dealt with, but it was a most unpleasant business while it lasted.

The Banda hut was so named because two brothers named Fowler spent a large amount of time on its preparation. They had been brought up as boys in Kenya where Banda was a common word for hut, apparently in the Swahili language, which they more or less insisted was the name by which the hut should be known. It has been called the Banda ever since. In the intervening years the Banda has been thoroughly modernised and is usually occupied by the leaders of the camps. It is also made available to Scripture Union workers when there is not a camp requiring its use.

New Swimming Pool

The first pool lasted for round about eleven years until money became available in 1958 for it to be replaced by another pool which was two and a half times bigger and much deeper.

The new pool was used for the first time on 21st June 1958; it apparently cost £259 and measured 28' x 14' and was 4' deep. It was made this size, not only for economy reasons, but also for maintenance purposes, which time has shown was the correct procedure. The pool was a great success and warmer than the previous one, but still on the cold side, while there is a photograph of a helper actually holding a kettle of boiling water which she is pouring into the cold water optimistically, though not realistically, with warming effectiveness in mind! It was put to abundant *use by the campers, not only for swimming though this was its principal function, but also for a thing called 'initiatives' which was meant to test the intelligence of the campers, and was a happening which belonged to nearly all the boys' summer camps.*

It was used for other purposes, too, notably the sailing of a coracle skilfully constructed by Tom Corkill, who was an expert bosun at many of the camps and whose children, now that he is happily married to Elizabeth, relish all the delights of Great Wood when they are able to attend.

Tents

There were always tents at Great Wood arranged most carefully around the edge of the camping field. Originally they were systematically hired from a firm near London who, when they eventually closed down around 1955, offered their regular customers a first choice of the goods that made up their residual stock. So, I went with Horace Webber to the warehouse and purchased six very good quality 12' x 12' tents and a number of tarpaulins at an attractive price. The tarpaulins were to cover the floors of the tents, but there were a number of additional ones which proved to be very useful in many ways, not least at camp fires, in order to provide protection for the campers when they sat on the ground which was often damp.

The purchased tents were extremely becoming; shaped like miniature marquees, they had walls which were not more than 5' or so high and a roof which was ingeniously supported with iron bars. Besides being good to look at the tents were exceptionally robust and ideal for sleeping two helpers or being a depository for the campers' suitcases and kit bags. They also had decorative dollies on the corners and on the pinnacles of their roofs.

I recall how this central dolly was forgotten on one occasion when the tent was erected. Instead of dismantling the whole tent, my daughter, who was small and active, was singled out to climb on its roof and attempt to place the dolly in position. She climbed on the roof all right but her foot went through the canvas, announcing the fact that the roof covering needed replacing. I do not remember what happened next. I only know that, from then on, at the end of the season usually, the canvas of the tents was

Cottage tents by Cabin 10

taken to a firm of restorers at Martock in Somerset named Yeo Brothers and Paul, who not only did any replacement that was needed [but] stored the canvas of the tents in a warehouse during the long winter months.

Journey Tents

When the senior camps were established at Great Wood the night journeys began. At the beginning these took place on the local hills, the senior campers involved sleeping out under the open sky. But the newsletter for Christmas some years later tells us that 1958 was one of the wettest years of camping remembered. It also carries a note that in future years bivouac tents will be used. This, then, must have been the year that the campers got soaking wet. The urgent drying out is well remembered but it is also recollected that none of the people concerned suffered from the experience. However, it was realised that lightweight tents must be used at all times. Eventually these tents, complete with flysheets, were ordered from Blacks of Greenock and the journeys which lasted for three days and two nights were transferred to the wide open spaces of Exmoor. There was a

31

light-hearted trial run on the Quantocks and I recall on a dry night going to bed in my sleeping bag under the stars in Butterfly Combe because all the tents were otherwise occupied.

For the main journeys, commencing on the outskirts of Exmoor, a coach was hired, and the complicated instructions worked out and given to the various groups by Rodney Musters in sealed envelopes, the campers being honour-bound not to open the envelopes before the specified timings. Each group had at least one trustworthy helper in charge who supervised this. The distance travelled and the intricacies of the tasks which had to be fulfilled were always according to the ages of the group. The journeys always finished at Lynmouth with a cream tea or its more solid equivalent.

A Lesson from the Jelly

John Axford, camper and leader from the 1950s, tells this true story:

'A distressed young Backwoodsman camper (aged about eleven) raced across the field to the camp commandant and blurted out, "Commy, Robert has sat in our jelly."' (Robert, whose name has been changed, was another boy in his cabin.)

'The commandant, whose experience with dealing with almost any emergency a camper might have was second to none, was temporarily at a loss on how to deal with this one ...

'To explain: it was the custom for each cabin group to cook their own lunch on their camp fire on one day during the camp. Although the first course was provided, it was up to the boys to choose and prepare the dessert. In this case, under the guidance of a very raw cabin officer, they decided on a multi-layered jelly concoction and proceeded as follows. First they looked round for a suitable receptacle, and one boy happened upon something they did not use very often – the bowl they used to wash in. This was set up on the cabin seat and during the few days before the lunch each layer of jelly was made and allowed to set before a different-flavoured next layer was added.

'All went well until the above unfortunate incident occurred. Thankfully, with the help of the cabin officer, the jelly was retrieved and the boys enjoyed their lunch.

'But, for that young cabin officer (and later camp leader), on prayerful reflection, this seemingly trivial incident left an abiding impression. A critical lesson was learnt which proved highly valuable in later years of both Great Wood camping and a professional career – today we call it risk management.

'"*The fear of the Lord is the beginning of wisdom, and they who live by it grow in understanding. Praise will be his name for ever.*" (Proverbs 111)

'(Worried parents please note that the washing bowl *was* thoroughly cleaned before use.)'

1960s: The Demise of the Nissen Hut

—⋄⊙⊙⋄—

*E*ventually the old Nissen hut and the boys' and girls' cabins were replaced with more sensitively designed new buildings, though this did not happen until the 1960s when the original buildings were wearing out, and money became available for their replacement. This concern for sensitive design has happily continued.

The fireplace built by Michael Phillips and Godfrey Scott-Mitchell not only provided warmth when necessary but also became a focal point for the hut when there were meetings. It lasted for thirteen years until one evening in 1960, almost to the day when it was built, without any warning, the brickwork of the chimney collapsed and disintegrated. The Crusader occupants of the Easter camp were inside the hut at the time so, fortunately, no one was hurt.

The collapse of the chimney confirmed the awareness already occupying the minds of those concerned and responsible that the moment was near for there to be serious thought about an entirely new building. By this time, everyone involved had grown very fond of the friendly Nissen hut, but it became a case of bowing to the inevitable. Therefore it was decided to launch an appeal to parents and old campers in June of 1961 for the cost of purchasing and erecting an adequate replacement.

The Nissen Replacement

The new hut was ready for use in 1962. It measured 56' x 26' and was sensitively designed by Michael Phillips. Michael made good use of the standard cedar wood modules manufactured by Vic Hallam of Nottingham and produced a most useful building. It was beautiful to look at and was well lit by numerous large windows. The complete concrete base for the area and roofing the space behind was done by a Spaxton builder named

Ingram. His firm also built a retaining wall of brickwork along the rearmost boundary. Mr Ingram also built an entirely new fireplace and chimney most attractively designed by Michael Phillips using brickwork within and a most pleasing random stone mixed with brickwork without.

The hut was partitioned inside as previously to form a kitchen and mess-hut-cum-meetings-and-activities area. There was a door and serving hatch connecting the two, while off the kitchen was a sizeable pantry, a ladies', and very welcome, rear-guard bathroom, a paraffin-fuelled (recently changed to Calor Gas) main hot water boiler, a large airing cupboard, and a section with a small table and a number of chairs for meals of those not eating with the camp. There still existed a large central table, a relic from the earliest days, which was used principally for the preparation and serving of meals; it had a familiar and most useful mechanical tin-opener permanently fixed at one end. [The table, with its original tin-opener, has been preserved and will be installed in the new 2018 mess hut kitchen, although some time ago it had to have a purpose-made stainless steel top added to meet current health regulations.] *Nowadays the Calor Gas needed for two cookers, a heated servery and the new hot-water boiler comes from a tank which has superseded the original cylinders because of their constant need of renewal. Eventually there was to be an electric water heater for the specific purpose of making hot drinks for all the members of the camp.*

Behind the new mess hut and under the lean-to roof was a wide passage with hooks on the hut wall for the purpose of hanging mackintoshes and anoraks in wet weather. It was reached by a most useful door at the rear of the building. There was also a front door on the right-hand side of the fireplace leading out to a patio where there were comfortable seats which always seemed to be in the sun. There are also side and back doors to the kitchen area.

On the far side of the wide passage and also under the new lean-to-roof there were to be the improved camp shop, two ablution areas with hot and cold running water, a shower and a large washing-up space. There was also to be a helpers' WC – this last had a door which was originally the front entrance to my house and was probably the only loo door in existence with a letter box! A considerable amount of work on all of these was done by the members of the Easter working parties in 1963 and 1964.

Opening the mess hut

The total cost of the new buildings, including the septic tank, was around £4,000 of which more than £2,500 was contributed by parents and old campers. The camp already had saved £1,000 which was in a special development account, while the outstanding amount was forthcoming in time to meet the bills.

The hut was opened on September 7th 1963 by Sir Alfred Owen, a memorable occasion which included an act of thanksgiving to God. It was attended by numerous parents and old campers. The day finished with a superlative camp fire at which Tony Dann, now grown up with an Oxford Blue, and a solicitor in his father's practice, made a most salutary speech.

The interior of the new hut was fittingly lined and painted while the partition on the mess hut side was subsequently covered with the three ply off-cuts from the interiors of the new cabins. The joins in the cladding were suitably covered with solid wooden framing in order to produce an effect of panelling. These most useful three ply off-cuts were opportunely rescued just in time as they were considered to be waste and were thrown out to be burnt. The heads and antlers of two red deer, which had adorned the Nissen hut, were fastened to the completed panelling.

The Coming of Electricity

It so happened when the new hut was being established that there was a rural development of mains electricity and that this was offered to camp. To begin with it was seriously considered to be a questionable amenity, likely to spoil the longstanding Backwoodsman traditions. Eventually, however, with acceptable assurances from the Electricity Board about the siting of poles and overhead cables, about which Dr John Laird, General Secretary of Scripture Union, was, fortunately, personally concerned, the electricity was warmly welcomed. The new hut was able to be wired during its erection while the mains electricity soon proved to be a boon in the kitchen, and was also beneficial in connection with meetings and activities for the use of projectors, tape recorders and suchlike.

Knowing the district I was able to gather together just the right quantity of disused but most becoming paraffin hanging lamps which were cleverly converted for electricity, in order to provide a sufficient number of lights for the mess hut, and thus doing away with the noisy Tilley pressure lamps. [These, too, are being installed in the new mess hut.] *The sleeping cabins, however, by the wishes of the campers, were to continue to be lit at night by the original paraffin storm lanterns. Certainly they were messy and unpredictable, though they were perfect for maintaining the ambience of the camp even when they smoked and stank.*

It so happened that I was visiting the camp in the early part of 1961 when the matter of the replacement of the Nissen hut was going forward. I was actually standing in the chapel clearing, probably meditating. Certainly I was thinking how splendid it would be if the open-air chapel could be provided with good weatherproof furniture. Then the significant thing happened, surely not by chance; it was decided to invite the expected donors to the cost of the new hut to allow a tenth of their gifts, as far as was needed, to be earmarked for such a purpose. A postscript to this effect was eventually added to the appeal letters, with the result that £250 became available, an adequate amount in those days.

A visit was made to Listers of Dursley in the Cotswolds, who were most co-operative and agreed to make the required number of comfortably wide teak benches especially without backs or arm-rests for the main body of the chapel. They also supplied a number of their standard seats for the rear and sides while two teak armchairs for the leader and speaker at the services,

37

Chapel in the snow

and a small slatted table, completed the order. A most beautiful lectern with a carving of the Scripture Union Lamp was constructed by a local craftsman named Bert Trout, while the workers of the Forestry produced a rough-hewn wooden cross, which was erected at the side of the clearing at the front. The precious portable organ, which had been at the camp almost from the beginning when it was played by David Gardiner with tremendous éclat, was carried across to give a lead to the singing.

So the open-air chapel was completely furnished in 1962 and a service, especially of the Lord's Supper or Holy Communion, in the natural surroundings, supported by the unending musical sound of the rippling stream, has to be experienced in order that its simple beauty may be fully realised.

Drainage

The drainage problem nevertheless was not yet resolved and John Rose, whose father had donated the water closets and who had done a surveying course as a part of his training as a builder, was given the task of inspecting the field. He came up with the opinion that most of the field was below the existing water table and that it would never drain properly until the present level was raised. This would be exorbitantly expensive but was nevertheless sensible as was shown by the land on which the new cabins were to be erected. At the same time that this was being undertaken, the new forestry road was being made. It was considerably wider and at a much higher level than the original one and passed the entrance to the camp. Adjustments had to be made and, as a form of compensation, I was able to persuade those concerned to dump a large quantity of hangman grit on the land where the new cabins were to be established. It was most successful and proved that John Rose was probably right.

Cabins

It was strongly felt that the campers' cabins, after doing sterling service for many years, should be substituted in 1965 by brand new buildings, not only in order to provide more comfort for the campers, but also to contribute to the appearance of the camp now that the improved main hut was satisfactorily established. At the same time it was felt that Cabin No. 1 should be left as it was, after its enlargement in 1953, while the new cabins could be sited in a row of six, directly opposite the main hut. Cabin No. 1 was to be given the fresh name of Old No. 1, and could be available as the sleeping quarters of helpers, now that these seemed to be on the increase. Cabin No. 10 was also to remain unaltered after its refurbishment in 1953.

The brand new cabins were architect designed by Michael Phillips, custom built, and erected by a firm named Pratten from Radstock in Somerset. The cabins were ready to be occupied at Easter 1965, although the Dunlopillo mattresses which were to be used on the eight two-tier bunks were some days late in arriving. These mattresses were purchased through a kind friend that I had at the firm of Dunlops, and although they were considered to be very good value for the price that had to be paid, they represented a considerable outlay. Their cost was wonderfully met by a timely and most generous gift from grateful parents in South Wales named Pratt. The members of the Easter working party were the first to use the new cabins and had to endure the hardness of the original mattresses, but did so without complaint. The original mattresses required considerable airing after their disuse during the winter months. This recurring chore was tiresome, equalled only, perhaps, by the renewing of the springs of

1965 cabins

many of the original bunks. These beds were noisy too, as the campers turned on them. All of this was to be a thing of the past with the new bunks which were strongly built into the structure of the cabins, and had solid wooden bases with no springs to be replaced. Shelves were also cunningly placed at the ends of the bunks for personal belongings. The rubber Dunlopillo mattresses were comfortable as well as attractive in that they required little airing after the winter. Each camper was also provided with a locker and a hanging space for clothes. Suitcases and other luggage were normally deposited in a special store for the duration of the camp. The lids to the lockers formed, as they had done in the previous cabins, ideal seats. Outside, under the overhanging roofs, were attractive permanent slatted benches for sitting in the sun.

Correct Nomenclature

I was, I am afraid, always a stickler for correct nomenclature. Cabins were cabins and not huts and certainly not sheds! An axe was an axe and not a chopper, while passing the test of its usefulness was called axemanship. The camp fire was to be called not a bonfire but a camp fire. One day a teasing camper said to me very politely, 'When you have finished supervising the bonfire, sir, will you please come to my hut and pass my chopmanship?'

Campers were divided into sides called Doones and Ridds after Blackmore's book, Lorna Doone. Common cries as a result of this were, 'Get rid (Ridd) of the Doones.' or 'Down (Doone) with the Ridds.' Small flags were made by the cooks in distinctive colours in order to distinguish between the two sides that always operated competitively against one another in the numerous activities of the camps. The first thing that the cabin leader was supposed to do, helped most probably by the cabin officer, was to erect a flag mast, which was always a work of skill. It incorporated cross trees, while there was a fixture on the cabin to which it could be fastened. Halyards and a pulley were available from the bosun of the camp. When it was all ready the camp burgee and the Doones' or Ridds' emblem were very proudly flown. There were additional burgees as well to denote skills in backwoodsmanship. These had to be earned by the members of the cabin. The chief of these burgees was for axemanship and concerned the safety rules and proper use of the axe, which was always kept prudently sharp. The test was extremely uncomplicated but had to be passed by every member of the group. The other tests were slightly less all-embracing in their requirements. The camp burgee could be forfeited when the points at daily inspection were very low. This was considered to be a great disgrace for the campers concerned, but very rarely happened.

There was always a light-hearted argument concerning the appellation of the little flags; some called them pennants while others called them burgees. Whatever they were called they always looked cheerful blowing in the wind, while at night time some campers ran up their lighted storm lanterns on the flag mast in place of the burgees, which had to be taken down when darkness fell and it was cocoa time. These burgees served a most useful purpose as well as looking elegant, because they conveyed to a camp helper or leader the skills in which the members of a cabin were proficient. The awarding of them belonged entirely to the province of the bosun, but they were regularly presented to the cabin members with great solemnity by the camp leader.

Tidiness

As well as being a stickler for correct nomenclature, I was very keen on the day-to-day tidiness of the camp, and with this I was greatly helped by a number of helpers, chief of whom was Michael Owen. Michael was a patrol leader in the original Scout camp from the junior school at Monkton Combe in 1943. He served in the regular army in different parts of the world when he left the senior school at Monkton in 1947, and was all ready to become my most excellent adjutant in the later years of the camps. He was eventually married to Pat Davies Shiel, one of Great Wood's most excellent cooks. God gave them four children who became my warm friends and helpers and campers at Great Wood after his time.

Discipline

I was, I believe, a strict disciplinarian as well, but Michael Owen is also remembered for saying that I always exercised this with a manifested love for the campers. Be that as it may be, I certainly most fervently believed that it was impossible to lead a camp or any other organisation for that matter in any other way. This applied to the helpers as well as to the boys and girls, while I probably erred by being too impatient with inefficiency. A favourite saying of mine was that I believed in the Divine right of leadership, which meant that I hoped I listened sympathetically to all that the helpers had to say on a given matter, but, having done so and weighed up the pros and cons, I made up my own mind as to what should be done. I was, as I saw it, the leader appointed by Camp's Headquarters, and felt most sincerely that to put any matter to the whim of a vote was a manifestation of breakdown in strategy.

Matushka Sarah Gascoigne, Frances Turner at the time, remembers an incident from one of the first Youth Focus camps in the sixties. 'We had been given a pep talk about getting to bed and respecting lights out. We had been assured that the officers would be vigilant that night in particular. Some of the more enterprising among us decided to put them to the test. Around ten o'clock one or two torches flashed a little between the girls' and boys' cabins near the back entrance. It took a while for them to notice, but we knew they had when two or three quickly rose and headed for the door. We left the camp, maybe twenty of us, and headed up the road, making sure to flash just enough light to keep them coming. We headed over the stream and back to the main entrance and into the mess hut where the plot was discovered. We all had a good laugh.'

Matushka is now an Orthodox priest's wife and, using her experience from Great Wood, has helped with an Orthodox camp in Oregon for many years.

Camp Fire

Behaviour at camp fire was strictly regulated. No eating or drinking was permitted during a normal fire. Campers, who mostly sat on the tarpaulins which were spread on the grounds, were not allowed to adopt a recumbent position; they were required to sit up in order to join in the singing. Occasionally, in the early days, camp prayers followed camp fire but this was eventually discontinued because of its unsuitability. In its place prayers always took place in the mess hut and preceded camp fire on the occasions when there was one. Prayers varied in length and followed a pattern of Bible teaching. They were certainly longer than the formal Taps at Scout or Guide camps, though it is hoped that they were not so long as to be burdensome. The camp prospectus made it clear that everyone should be present. There were usually no prayers in the morning at Great Wood. It was felt that the morning session of Bible reading in cabin groups with a provision for private prayers was sufficient.

The camp fire itself was usually pagoda-shaped with brushwood packed into the sizeable pieces of wood that formed the framework. These were meticulously cut into the correct sizes by the builders. It really was a work of art, and always seemed to require a vast amount of wood for which the nearby forest seemed to provide a never-ending supply. At one juncture the fires, built principally by Derek Joy, had to be reduced in size as they were too hot by far when they properly got going. They were lit by two responsible junior helpers using long torches soaked in paraffin, commonly called 'fire water' by the campers.

Camp fire

Entertainment at the camp fire was relaxed and of a very high quality. The camp song was invariably sung while the songs which followed were highly supportive. Simple favourites, which everybody got to know by heart, come readily to mind. They include 'Henry My Son', 'In the Woods There Was a House', 'My Hat It Has Three Corners'; this last was always sung first of all in English and then in German! Many of the songs had sensible actions which would gradually take over the song being sung so that in the end it was almost entirely actions. Some of the ditties were popular rounds. 'Going on a Lion Hunt', which was dramatically recited, line after line, following the leader, was a great favourite. Quite often a cabin would perform a 'Stunt', and many of these 'Stunts' were very good indeed. There was regularly a prayer to finish the proceedings which purposefully reminded those present of the teaching which had taken place earlier in the evening at proper camp prayers. Then it was back to the mess hut for cocoa which could be brought out and drunk in quietness in the gathering darkness by the dying embers of the camp fire.

Flag Break

Mention must also be made of flag break, which occurred in the mornings before breakfast at all the summer and Whitsuntide camps. It was an informal affair but served the realistic purpose of making sure that all the campers were up and dressed and ready for Quiet Time in the cabins. On some occasions at the summer camps boys would come to this unconventional parade dressed in pyjamas with bathing trunks underneath, all ready to be thrown into the swimming pool, in which many of them delighted. The proceedings continued, with the 'offenders' dealt with in a light-hearted manner when flag break was over. The Union Jack was 'broken' at the top of the flag-mast while the helpers and campers stood at the 'alert' in a circle around it. A ration of biscuits was issued when the assembly was 'easy all' and any notices, or nonsense rhymes, recited while these biscuits were being eaten. Then it was camp groups as soon as possible for the Scripture Union Bible reading for the day, followed by a private and personal prayer time. Breakfast came next and the busy day began.

'The day came,' writes John Simmons, 'when SU's head office decided that Great Wood needed to be brought up to date, nomenclature changed, and some of the traditions discontinued. They sent a member of staff to Youth Focus on an overnight visit to see what went on. When asked what he would like to see the next day, he replied that he would just join in with whatever we did, and I explained the day started with flag break. This normally consisted of merely raising the flag first thing, properly folded so it would "break" at the mast head (preferably without an egg concealed within). Peter Barker, who was Adjy that year, went round each cabin that evening and prepared the campers for a more formal occasion, so that, exactly ten minutes after Reveille, he blew the horn and each cabin marched across the field in turn and stood to attention at the flagpole. It wasn't until Pete called, "Cooks forward," and the cooks marched across the field with rolling pins on their shoulders that the poor chap from SU realised he had been had!'

Days' Programmes

Often there was an excursion to the local hills, almost certainly with Ordnance map work and orienteering, which were specialities of John Axford, a regular and valued member of the team as quartermaster in the summer; he also attended the working party camps over the Easter bank holidays, where he excelled at carpentry. He also led one of the Backwoodsman camps very expertly with David Mitchell when I left Great Wood in 1971. David Mitchell was most excellent too.

Sometimes there was an outing by coach to Dunster and Minehead. The last named had the two-fold attraction of an extremely pleasant swimming pool and a funfair where the dodgems were the principle source of appeal. On one notable occasion a certain lady cook mistook a strange boy for a camper and most generously paid for his ride! The excursion to Minehead almost invariably finished with a visit to Blue Anchor Bay, so called, apparently, for the colour of its mud, though the mud always seemed to be black in colour and exceedingly sticky, especially at low tide if, as happened occasionally, some extrovert camper was attracted by it. If the tide was high enough a second swim was in order, while the non-swimmers paid a most rewarding visit to the Alabaster Rocks or went off hopefully to collect fossils. There was always an excursion further afield to Exmoor with a long walk, helped in its final stages by the coaches, and usually finishing up at Lynmouth with a cream tea or its equivalent for which tokens were issued by the camp.

All these excursions needed a packed lunch. Sandwiches for this were made with different kinds of spread at the breakfast table. This was done in order that the campers could choose their favourite spread. In this connection a not too apt though favourite metaphor was often used: 'Having made your bed, it is you who has to lie on it.' Paper bags were issued for the lunches, and the individual was instructed to write his or her name on them. Hard-boiled eggs, and cake, and fruit were often supplied as well. There was also a cooked meal in camp in the evening to follow these quite often long excursions. When there was not an excursion there would often be an afternoon activity in camp such as rag sports or 'initiatives', which have been already mentioned. On these occasions the mornings were free for games or passing tests or simple private pleasures. There was a tradition at Great Wood that all participants in the camp should have free time and be encouraged to use it beneficially.

BW 1976	MORNING	AFTERNOON	EVENING
FRI. 23RD JULY	OFFICERS MEETING, 09.30	ARRIVAL BUS LEAVES TAUNTON – 17.00	SUPPER PRAYERS – J.A.
SAT 24TH	IN CAMP	WIDE GAME	PRAYERS
SUN 25TH	MORNING CHURCH	ORG. HILL WALK OR GAME	HYMNS FILMSTRIP
MON 26TH	HILLS LEAVE – 11.30	WALK RETURN 16.00	PRAYERS
TUES 27TH	IN CAMP	INITIATIVES.	PRAYERS
WED 28TH	EXCURSION WOOKEY HOLE LEAVE 10.00	RETURN LEAVE 15.30	PRAYERS
THURS 29TH	IN CAMP	COMPASS EXERCISE ENDING ON HILLS	PRAYERS
FRI 30TH	LEAVE – 10.00 EXMOOR	LEAVE LYNMOUTH 18.00	SHORT PRAYERS (FILMSTRIP)
SAT 31ST	IN CAMP CAMP SITE LUNCH	IN CAMP	PRAYERS CAMP FIRE
SUN 1ST AUG.	CAMP SERVICE – 11.00	PAIDER TENNIS FINAL CLEAR-UP	FILM STRIP OR SLIDES PRIZEGIVING
MON 2ND	DEPARTURE CLEAR-UP BUS LEAVES – 08.45	'NET MENDING'	DINE

Camp programme

47

When Mike Menzies, camper and team from the 1960s, was a camper at B Camp, they used to go to Butlin's at Minehead for a day out. 'One year, around 1962, I won a china pig at the shooting gallery. I still use it to collect my foreign coins when I come back from abroad. I would like to think this is what prompted my nickname "Piggy" at Great Wood, but I fear it is actually my large appetite.'

Radios

In the 1960s, as far as Bill Carter is aware, there was just one radio allowed on camp, which was situated in the Banda and was for the exclusive use of Mrs I. 'Without radios, televisions or newspapers (and long before mobile phones or the internet), campers and team existed in a news-free bubble. There was just one exception. At the end of the notices after lunch and after the evening meal, Mrs I would stand up and tell us the latest cricket test match score (and there always seemed to be a game at some stage during camp)!'

Fog on the Hills

During a map reading exercise on the hills (now called orienteering), David Fieldsend, camper and team from the 1960s, remembers the fog coming down. A plaintive voice came from nearby out of the fog: 'I can't find Wilmot's Pool,' followed by a loud splash and then 'I've found it now!'

Sundays

It has also to be admitted that Sunday was often an uncertain day in the camps. Everything was done at the official Scripture Union Camps to make the day extra special, and there was always an emphasis on good food at meal times. The beginnings of the day were effectual enough. There was a morning service in camp, or else all the members visited the local Anglican village churches at either Nether Stowey or Over Stowey, which eventually formed a united benefice and had a lively evangelical vicar. Everyone was expected after siesta to walk in the forest in the afternoon. There was hymn singing in the mess hut after high tea, which took the place of camp prayers. A form of occupation for the Sunday afternoon was to find a good deer's slot and take a plaster cast of it. The only trouble was that good deer's slots were few and far between except in wet weather when it was comparatively simple, in muddy places, to discover where the deer had been and to take a suitable cast of its footprints provided one had the right materials. These were readily available from the bosun at the camp who was also prepared to instruct the campers, if necessary, about the correct procedures to follow for success. Wise members not only listened carefully, but anticipated all that they needed and went fully prepared. The waiting time while the wet plaster of Paris dried was never of considerable length, and allowed ample time for the campers concerned to get back in time for high tea.

Riding Accident

John Axford recalls that at the Youth Focus camp of 1968, JI had taken a group of boys riding when one young lad raced ahead. JI could see the overhanging branches coming up so chased after him to lead the run-away horse away from danger. He succeeded in doing this but in the process came off his own horse and suffered a number of broken ribs. As a result of his injuries he was unable to return to that camp and Michael Owen led the rest of it.

A Timely Invitation

David Whitehouse, now a trustee of GWT, first came to Great Wood in the summer of 1968. 'Before that,' he says, 'I had heard several of my friends talking about this place that they went to in the summer down in the Quantocks, but I had never thought that this would be something for me. However, in 1968 I was at my confirmation retreat which was being led by John Inchley. For whatever reason, JI felt it right to offer me an invitation to come to Great Wood that summer.

'I will never forget the sense of excitement as the coach made its way up the combe towards the front gate of camp. Even after all this time there is still a definite frisson as I approach this wonderfully beautiful place nearly fifty years later.

'The times spent at Great Wood as camper, senior camper, junior officer and officer were all packed with experiences and the making of friendships, many of which have lasted to the present day. Attending the work party and, latterly, running this over the Easter weekend has meant that I have been able to be at Great Wood for some part of the year for every single year since that first, wonderful summer.'

Through the Eyes of a Young Person

'What do I remember of Great Wood as a child of a member of the team?' John, Michael Owen's son, asks. 'Most people remember the sun shining as a child, but my memories of Great Wood have a lot of rain in them – although not in a bad way! I had an underlying feeling of always feeling very much at home at Great Wood, and remember a lot of late teens/twenties role models, who probably got too much of my attention, but on the positive side many are very good friends now.

'I remember, when I was about seven, the adventure camp boys about to head out on a walk. It was chucking it down with rain. I insisted I wanted to go. My dad tried unsuccessfully to persuade me it would not be fun. Somehow I got my way. By the top of Ashley Combe I was drenched and feeling very sorry for myself. Peter Buchanan was detailed to take me back to camp. I seem to remember jogging back down Ashley Combe and feeling very glad to get back to camp. I then remember everyone else's return later in the day and JI telling the campers they could have a shower but it was limited to one minute per camper!

'I and my siblings joined in with quite a lot, but usually as add-ons to leaders rather than joining in with the campers. We had quite a bit of choice about whether we joined in or not. It was a very privileged position to be in and I loved it – to the extent that the thought of being a "proper" camper maybe held less appeal.'

Saying Goodbye

JI writes:

There was also a tradition in my time of saying goodbye to the campers and helpers. Outside the gates of the camp was a most convenient hillock on which the participants would stand in order to do this. There was always one who was armed with a hunting horn, principally my daughter, Rosemary, when she was old enough. On this horn would be blown the sorrowful dirge, which the huntsman while following the stag or hind was always loath to blow: the sad call of 'Gone Away'. It always made a fitting end to the camps while the scene makes a fitting enough ending to this Story of Great Wood, and of God's provision for the camps which have been held constantly since 1943, and are still being held under the Scripture Union banner. The story continues and probably will never end, while God still provides. We all need to remember that the purpose of writing thus is to acknowledge God's goodness and ascribe to him all the glory for the mighty things he has done. In the early years someone parodied a New Zealand Maori folk song:

> *Now is the time when we must say goodbye,*
> *Soon we'll be leaving the forest and the hill,*
> *While you're away, remember Great Wood Camp,*
> *When you return you'll find a welcome still.*

Or, as two campers named Stephen Johnson and Patrick Musters wrote the day before they were due to leave 'B' camp in 1964,

> *Oh! Let us stay, just a little bit longer,*
> *Oh! Let us stay, just another day more,*
> *Now camp is over, we hope to meet again.*
> *We would like to stay, but we have to go away,*
> *Tomorrow, tomorrow, let tomorrow never come.*

1970s: New Leaders as John Inchley Leaves

Schools Work

Derek Briggs was the manager of Great Wood for Somerset County Council's use of the camp between 1967 and 1981.

Michael Briggs, his son, recalls, 'I frequently accompanied him to the camp, spending a great deal of time exploring the surrounding forest while he worked, as well as swimming in the (old) pool from time to time. Apart from the water feeling close to freezing point, my other memory of the pool is inserting a stick into one of the pipes feeding the pool and receiving a fright when a frog jumped out at me! Later, as a teenager and as a Scout very well practised in constructing rope bridges and other structures, I built Great Wood's first "adventure area" by the stream as an upgrade to the single Tarzan rope that had, until then, been the main method of accidentally getting wet.

'My mother, Pat Briggs, never lets me forget another incident that occurred while we were helping out at a teacher training weekend at the camp. She and Derek's cousin Margaret Middle were running the catering in the kitchen, while my brother and I served at the tables. The dessert on this particular day was one giant-sized fruit flan per table. As I approached the edge of the table my grip on the tray wavered. Carried by my forward momentum and the angle of the tray, the flan escaped – right way up – onto the table and proceeded to slide along, coming to rest in front of the very surprised and somewhat alarmed teachers at the far end!

'It was to introduce the teachers to the educational possibilities available that Derek ran the teacher training weekends at Great

Wood. He very much viewed his work as a vocation rather than a job, and I'm certain that he wouldn't have been paid for extras like teacher training weekends – which is no doubt why the extended family were co-opted to help out.

'Pat also recalls that one of the male teachers had been out doing activities all morning and had remarked that one of his wellington boots wasn't very comfortable. As he took them off at lunch time to investigate, a blue tit flew out!

'Pat was also involved in the Guiding movement and in 1980 held a forty-eight-hour "sponsored sing" around the Great Wood camp fire for a weekend, with the Brownies mostly singing by day, and the Guides by night. Apart from having to collect a great deal of wood from the forest, it was enjoyed by all and raised a useful amount of money.

'Both Derek and Pat were also instrumental in launching the Campbell Room as another group accommodation option, further down the valley from Great Wood. John Inchley had held camps there during the Easter holidays before the establishment of a permanent Great Wood camp.

'In Derek's time the educational focus at Great Wood was mainly focused on environmental sciences and local studies – wildlife, geography, geology, the rural economy and the like; as well as being a former science teacher Derek was (among other things) a geologist, field biologist and mountain leadership trainer. While the schools chose their own programmes (normally with his guidance), most of them were primary schools and the teachers weren't normally specialists in such areas, so most of them opted to have him lead such activities for much of their stay, and to make use of the minibus that he drove, as well as his contacts with the Forestry Commission, local farms, and businesses such as the farrier and baker in Over Stowey. I believe that it wasn't unusual for a week at Great Wood to provide enough material and ideas for a school to continue to work on Great Wood-inspired topics for several weeks after their return.

Derek in action

'When the SU were in residence he also spent time visiting schools pre-and-post-visit as well as working at the other County Council centres – Kilve Court, Pinkery and Charterhouse, and (for one term) at Dieppe, France.'

Promotional Attire

'In the early 1970s,' Mike Menzies recalls, 'Richard Dunn and I were helping at the Backwoodsman camp. We both came to one camp with the first ever "Great Wood Camp" T-shirt. Mine had letters ironed on which lasted many years until one of the letters wore off. I still have the T-shirt but now it just reads "Great Woo Camp". Seems rather appropriate.

'Around this time I was helping look after the swimming pool. In those days we had a spring which fed water to the camp and to the pool. But if the pool was short of water we could divert water from the old concrete milk churn pond (in the stream behind

Cabin 3 – it's still there). However, taking water from the stream often drew fine grit from the stream into the pool. So one dry summer I was able to borrow a stocking from Margaret Buchanan to act as a filter or strainer. I'm not sure I ever gave it back!

'Talking of the milk churn, do you remember who it was who, when told to go and put the milk in the stream, went and poured all the milk out of the churn into the stream? Maybe this should remain in the mists of time!'

Easter Antics

Bill Carter found the work party drew him as a teenager. 'I think it was because, as a boarder, none of my school friends were around at home over Easter, whereas many very good non-school friends were at Great Wood. It was also a chance to give something back to a place that was very special for me.

'On one occasion I was working with Rodney Musters trying to extract a wooden stake sunk well into the ground by the bosun's store. After an initial tug at it when we failed even to make it quiver, Rodney suggested we apply some physics. I hadn't a clue what he meant. "Levers, mechanical advantage – you know about that?" Yes, I did, but I had never thought about applying it! A log pole and a short piece of rope strategically placed made all the difference. It was to be a well learned lesson.

'At another work party Richard Hallett was busy clearing the accumulated winter debris from the roof of the mess hut when he stepped too much to one side of the supporting timbers over the rear section. The result was that he fell through the roof of the shop. Mercifully someone at the end of the previous season had thought to store the lightweight camping tents just there and it was on these that he landed. Richard, whilst mildly shaken, was unhurt and the first anyone else knew of it was him knocking on the inside of the shop door, asking to be let out!

'In the 1960s and 1970s the shop sold Corona fizzy drinks in

Corona lorry

glass bottles. As a senior camper one of the pre-camp tasks was to help unload the Corona lorry when it arrived and store the crates under the counter in the shop. To make the task easier the lorry driver would come across the field to get as close to the shop as possible. Is it just my imagination or did the lorry get stuck on numerous occasions? However many times it was, it seemed just another part of the pre-camp routine to help push him out of whatever had snared him.

One Thing Leads to Another

Janice Baines, as she was at the time, remembers, 'I arrived at Great Wood in the summer of 1969, aged eleven, having been invited by Commy when he came to our church. He led the last Mixed B camp before the girls' camps began. Great Wood became a place of acceptance and belonging for me, a place where I could be myself.

'I continued to come, progressing to Youth Focus where a senior camper, Richard Dunn, got me on the cooking team for adventure camp at age fifteen, though I pretended to be eighteen! There I met a camper, Dave Morris.

'Dave and I worked on many camps over the years and were married by John Inchley in 1981. We continued to come to Youth Focus, helping to lead for a number of years. Dave is a Baptist minister and we recognise that our ministry is rooted in the continuity and stability of God's work through Great Wood.

'Last August 2017, we brought our eldest grandson to Escape – the third generation of our family to attend camps at Great Wood. What a privilege!'

In with the New and Out with the Old

In 1973 the JI hut was built.

A small work party including Alan Martin, Peter Hudson, David Whitehouse, Liz Lauste, Bill Carter and Bill's sister Sue arrived on site to do a few final bits of fitting out. Bill recalls that for reasons

JI hut

perhaps known to some, but not to many, the bunks in the corner rooms had been built with the upright three-by-three-inch timbers on the outside of the structure rather than the inside. This meant that the space to hold the mattresses was six inches narrower all round. As the plan had been to have a small space at the end of the bed for personal belongings the decrease in length was not so critical, but the width was a different matter. One of the tasks that weekend was to remove the Dunlopillo mattresses from their covers and cut a six-inch strip off each – more difficult than it sounds.

Another of the tasks, which went like a house on fire, was burning the old middle hut, which had been reduced to a haphazard pile of wall and roof panels. Years of careful creosoting had ensured that once started there was no stopping the fire. Bill Carter remembers flinging on one panel and watching in fascination as the Georgian wired glass window simply sagged with the intense heat and dripped molten glass into the flames. Once the fire had died down enough to approach more slowly, the old piano was also committed to the flames.

'At the start of one summer camp,' Bill says, 'before the boys arrived, a few of the team who had arrived early were enjoying lunch in the kitchen when they became aware of strange noises in the passage by the shop. We went to investigate and were surprised to find that a horse had come inside. We attempted to push it out as there wasn't room for it to turn round, but discovered just how heavy, and stubborn, a horse can be. Fortunately for us at that point Derek Briggs arrived and in no time the horse was back where it belonged in the fresh air.

'With JI's retirement in 1971 the life of Great Wood took on a different feel. Instead of having one person overseeing all the camps, each camp now had its own leader. Whilst a number of these leaders had come to camps with JI as leader themselves and therefore tended to carry on a number of the traditions (flag break, camp fire songs, lion hunts, carving the Sunday roast, to name a

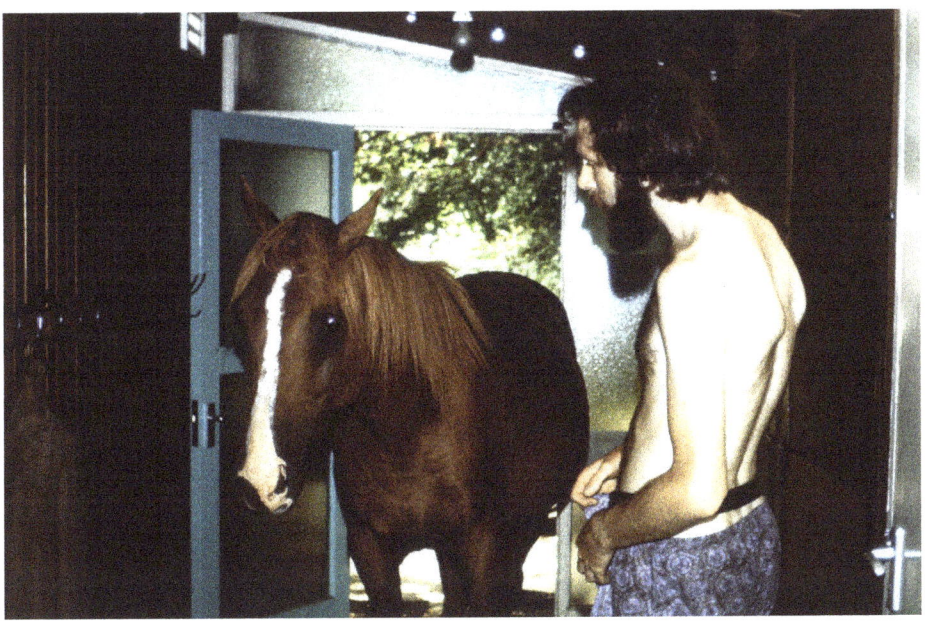

John Weaver confronting the horse

few), this was not always the case. The camps began to diversify. The boys' camps made small changes to the traditional programme whilst the girls' camps experimented much more. The common element, however, remained the forging of lasting friendships, the nurturing by the senior leaders of the junior team members and the amazing sense of unity as we worshipped and served God together in a very special place.'

Happily Ever After

Elizabeth Weaver (née Cunningham), camper and team from the 1960s, recalls, 'On Easter Sunday 1976 during a walk around Great Wood following lunch, John Weaver proposed to me. We sat on a log and I cried but said yes. That evening during the meeting, Michael Owen asked for people to share news and John said that he had asked me to marry him. The room exploded with cheers!

'We were married on 21st August 1976 following the Backwoodsman camp, so I didn't get JI hut married quarters.

'Forty-one years later and we are still enjoying Great Wood.'

Tradition and Transport

Sylvia Fox recalls a lot of 'fab' times from 1976 till well into the 1980s, when work got too much to take annual leave for camp. 'Camp is still very important to me – and a somewhat mad tradition has grown up, where every vehicle I own (can't call them cars, as they are elderly MPVs for godchildren/parish transport or camper vans or similar) is driven to camp within its first year. It feels as if it is a place of blessing the ministry that the vehicle will have. The first long solo drive was, naturally, to camp, the summer I qualified driving, and it has continued ever since.

'I remember being at camp for Easter – the only time I have ever been away from our own church for Easter Day – and being amazed when we got given Creme Eggs at St Mary's in the service. I also did the pool length swim challenge later in the day to get another one!

'We once were on a coach going to the beginning of a walk (or coming back – I forget which), when the driver took a short cut – and got us stuck on a ninety-degree corner in Over Stowey. It took about thirty minutes to get free, but I think the driver managed not to damage the cottage.'

David Whitehouse also recalls an incident with the coaches. 'We had spent a day on Exmoor – yet another beautiful part of the West Country – and were returning back to camp by coach from Lynmouth. Those who remember the old semi-automatic coaches will recall how much they seemed to struggle up Countisbury Hill and this year was no exception. In fact, on this particular journey the struggle proved too much and the coach came to a smoking halt halfway up the hill. Surprisingly no one seemed to be at all bothered by this, reckoning that the coach company would make the necessary arrangements for getting us all back safely to Great Wood. Conversations sprang up all around the coach discussing the recent talks that we had heard at camp and how much God's beauty had been seen all around us during the day.

'Eventually a replacement coach arrived and we did, indeed, return safely to camp. However, the story does not end there as many of those who had been on the coach had been touched by the conversations and continued these in the Great Wood chapel. How much God is in control, even in something as mundane as a coach breakdown, can be seen from the fact that several people gave their lives to Christ that day – something that may not have happened had this extra hour or so of questions and discussion not been made available in this way. "How great Thou art" indeed!'

A Very Memorable Work Party

'I remember Michael Owen and David Mitchell sitting with me in the chapel on Easter Day 1976, the same day John and Elizabeth Weaver became engaged,' Mike Menzies says. 'Though I was more than comfortable with Jesus, they helped me with my doubt about the existence of God. So I committed myself to the Christian way and have been so for over forty years. But that's not all. I was also asked to look after Gehenna.[1] Combustion seemed to suit me and I have had a career in furnaces and heat transfer for the same forty years. Some say I have just been covering my options so that if I don't get into heaven at least I'll get a good job down below.

'At Backwoodsman camp it was quite popular to go deer stalking early in the morning, after dawn, before flag break. One day I was with three campers walking on the edge of the forest

---

[1] Gehenna is mentioned in the Bible as the Place of Burning and so was adopted as the name for the Great Wood rubbish incinerator.

when a fawn suddenly broke cover from the edge of the path on which we were walking. She tried to escape into the field next to the forest but got caught in the fence. I stooped down and picked her up and put her down on the other side of the fence. She ran off and returned through a gap in the fence a few hundred yards further on and disappeared into the forest.'

A Lifetime of Memories

Gill Wood (now Hollis) first saw Great Wood in 1972 when she went to pick up her big sister, who was the only camper left on site.

'While Mum and Dad talked with the officers, Jenny showed me round,' she says. 'The swimming pool was empty, so we slid around on the bottom in the slime! Then we were invited for lunch in the kitchen with the team. When someone got up to answer the phone another team member stole their plate and we passed it under the table between ourselves. I thought this was brilliant but my sister was really embarrassed. I couldn't wait to be eleven so that I could go back there.

'My first two camps were in the long, hot summers of 1975 and 1976. I remember a first-night thunderstorm while we were walking in the woods; ponies bumping into the cabin walls during the night; swinging on the rope hanging over the stream; walking on Exmoor. And learning new songs: "Seek Ye First" and "A New Commandment" were my favourites.

'On one occasion, we met a group of teenage boys at the picnic site and one of my cabin invited them back to camp! This terrified the rest of the cabin and the male members of the team were sent to patrol the edge of the site to make sure there were no random boys. Chris Hey arrived back at Cabin 2 looking flushed and nervous, saying he thought he had heard a boy in the bushes in the chapel ... but actually it was a hedgehog.

'On the last night we had a midnight feast ... not in secret in the cabin but in the tent of our cabin officer. Her twin sister was one of the cooks and she brought us toast.'

Elizabeth Carter (née Gibson) recalls that the first girls' camps had no male team, and at the Gibson twins' eighteenth birthday there was a long discussion about all the valuable roles a male team could play. 'I may have had the ulterior motive of bringing Bill Carter to camp! However, Joan (later known as Joy) Young was gracious enough to allow a trial in 1976, and Chris Hey and David Whitehouse were the pilots. Despite my hopes, Bill had a summer university course to attend!'

Another Camp Is Born

Over a cup of tea in the mess hut in summer 1976, Margaret Buchanan (now Ferguson) commented to Sybil Green from SU that it was sad that the twelve-year-old girls would have to miss a year before they would be old enough to attend the Youth Focus camp at Easter. Margaret didn't give it another thought until she was contacted during the autumn and told that they had made space during the summer for a second girls' camp for thirteen- and fourteen-year-olds, and would she run it? They met to discuss the way forward for what was to become the girls' adventure camp, and only towards the end of the 'interview' (if you can call it that) was she asked, 'By the way, how old are you?' There was much relief when she replied, 'Twenty-six,' because the minimum age at that time for camp leaders was twenty-five. For the next seven years it was over to Margaret! How things have changed!

Gill Hollis recalls lying in bed after lights out at this new camp, discussing the male members of the team with the other girls. 'I like Rob,' said one. 'I quite like Bill,' said another. 'Thank you very much,' came Bill's voice from outside. The lookout on the top right bunk had not been doing her job properly!

Then in 1979 Gill graduated to Youth Focus at Easter. 'One of my fondest memories is crawling through the undergrowth of the forest during a wide game, trying to get back to camp without being spotted. The officer in charge was taking it so seriously. And bird watching ... we saw one bird. And the Great Wood book of records, where my name appeared three times: once for plastic cup tearing (into over a hundred pieces), for Polo mint sucking (twenty-eight minutes (I think) until it broke) and for the longest basket during the Cumberland Square Eight. No one who has ever danced that at Great Wood will forget the guys diving through the hatch or the partners running all round the outside of the mess hut to get back in time for their next turn.'

The Kitchen

Sue Nicholls (now Keighley) first helped in the kitchen at camp at Youth Focus in 1979 along with Sarah Hurding, Ruth Darrah and Susie Trapnell. 'One of our jobs as junior cooks was to cut the bread for fried bread for breakfast. The bread was cooked by Wilf, the local baker. He would turn up early each morning, come up the stairs to the kitchen door and put the bread into a large metal bread bin to the left (where the hand wash sink was latterly). The bread bin was next to the milk churn which we would take down to the farm to have filled up from the milking parlour every morning. I feel blessed to have known such innocence.

'Back to the fried bread! The idea was to cut the loaves into eight along the length and three across – we would use three loaves and thus have seventy-two large bread wedges. These were then put into a plastic bag and left overnight to become a bit stale so that they would fry better in the morning. Bring on the Trex! They would be served with sausages, beans, tomatoes or scrambled eggs.

'I have much to thank the bread for. Mary Murray was the cook that year, ably assisted by Colin, her husband, as quartermaster. I think that us four junior cooks caused her a few headaches. However, I don't think that it was down to us that she decided it was time to retire from cooking at camp. John and Jan Simmons asked her if there was anyone who could take over and she said that none of us was much good (hugely ironic as Ruth is now an amazing cook!), but that at least I could cut bread straight. The next year I took over as cook and my heart has never left the Great Wood kitchen.'

At the Backwoodsman camp in 1977 there were four cooks. Jane Senior was pregnant and so a number of smells made her stomach uneasy. She would frequently comment that something smelled off and seek confirmation. Elizabeth Weaver would take a sniff and agree. They would ask the opinion of the two more junior cooks, Elizabeth Gibson (now Carter) and Morag Scott, who both thought the product (normally milk or meat) was fine but didn't want to upset the more senior ladies. It caused a bit of tension. It was a few weeks after camp finished when Elizabeth Weaver discovered that she also had been pregnant during camp. They have laughed a lot about it since.

A Parent Recalls

Sue Keighley's mother, Ruth Nicholls, recalls, 'When our daughter was eleven years old she went off to the SU girls' camp at Great Wood. It was a wet week and on her return her wellies (compulsory) were caked in mud. Her father cleaned them for her, only to be greeted by wails of dismay: "But, Daddy, that was GREAT WOOD MUD."

'That camp was the first of many, and Youth Focus, Storm and ski trips to Austria and France followed. Her brother, Neil, was introduced to camp as soon as he was old enough and he enjoyed Backwoodsman before joining Sue at the teenage events. Eventually they became junior officers and Sue began her contributions as cook at many camps.'

Mary Gibson also had several children spend a lot of time at Great Wood and she learnt that they always needed sleep and food before you asked the question 'How was camp?'! Then you couldn't stop them. Camps gave children brought up in Christian homes the chance to be themselves and think about the big issues of life for themselves, she explains. They played a vital role in self-commitment and action.

1980s: The Gate Bootiful

'The name "Great Wood", especially to those who stay at the site during the winter and spring months, is almost synonymous with "red mud",' Bill Carter says. 'How many of us have tried in vain to remove the Great Wood stains from our clothes? And of course it is a constant battle during wet camps to keep the mud out of the various buildings. It was to help with this that an extension was built on to the shop end of the mess hut in 1980 to act as a mud trap. The walls were fitted with shelves large enough to take wellington boots and there was a section of raised floor leading inwards on which muddy footwear was not allowed. Along the edge of the raised area was a strip of wood with "V" notches cut into it to facilitate removing boots without the need to get hands muddy. All in all a well-designed space. It was

Mess hut with Gate Bootiful

nicknamed "The Gate Bootiful", which, like the mud itself, has stuck.'

Stars in Their Eyes

The dates of the Backwoodsman camp are always close to the Perseid meteor shower. The lack of artificial light in Quantock Combe also makes it a good viewing point. So it was that the team were talking about the meteors when one of the cooks, Hilda Carter, confessed that she had never seen a shooting star. Naturally Mike Menzies offered to guide her up the combe after the campers had lights out. He was chatting in the mess hut when one of the team came in: 'Mike, Hilda is waiting for you outside the mess hut.' He rushed out and invited her to walk up to Blue Butcher's cottage (of which more in appendix 1). Because it was dark he held her hand. They stopped at the cottage and it was also quite cool, so he put an arm around her shoulder. Well, Hilda never did see a shooting star because she had her eyes closed all the time. They were married, of course, in 1982.

'Do you remember the Belfast sinks in the kitchen?' Mike Menzies asks. 'We were all getting ready for the swell dinner on the last night of camp. One of the cooks, Hilda, was wearing a dress! But this exposed her knees, which, by the last day of camp, were looking the worse for wear. So the ladies stood her in the sink and washed her knees and feet until they were a suitable colour for attending our swell dinner.'

Elizabeth Carter adds that there are many pictures too of the small children of team members being bathed in the Belfast sinks in the days before a formal bathroom. 'Those children are now grown up and have refused permission for the photos to be printed!'

'Children of team on site became a regular feature, which was necessary if we were to enable team members to come back when they had become parents,' Gill Hollis observes. 'The small children often acted as a valuable safe haven for youngsters struggling with homesickness or just not finding making friends so easy. They were allowed an incredible amount of freedom, but everyone on site would watch out for them.'

One example of this, which Mike Menzies remembers, was when a young girl set off to explore Great Wood on her own. Her mummy had said to her, 'Don't go into the bog.' (There is an unkempt soggy area at the top of the field, somewhat recovered these days, particularly with the low ropes course.) So Nicola Whitehouse wandered round, followed the stream, and then found an area which seemed to demand to be explored – tall trees, long grass, hedgerow shrubs reaching out to claim the territory. The light broke through the undergrowth in places to give the area even more fascination. The foliage added quietness. The rest of the world seemed to have moved away. But, as is common with situations near the boundaries between goodness and danger, Nicola began to get into difficulty. Not only were the trees overwhelming her and the hedgerows reaching out for her, but also the long grass had given way to an ever-tightening quagmire. Nicola was in trouble. Her calls for help were smothered by the bush and overwhelmed by the wind rustling through the branches. But, as Nicola's hopes were fading like her voice, a friendly woodman (Mike) heard her pleas. Striding as fast as the bog would allow him, he scooped up the young girl into his strong arms and forged a path to the open field and safety!

Judy Hunt ran the girls' adventure camp after Margaret and she recalls the head cook, Audrey Stanley (now Dixon), being really worried when she heard that some people from SU 'head office' were coming, as she'd got in quite a quantity of scrumpy and thought they might assume she was plying the girls with alcohol. It was actually for the pork main course of the banquet (a real highlight of the camp) and all the alcohol was 'cooked off' in the process. Visits from SU staff were a regular feature; they formed a good opportunity for office-based staff to see what was happening at the grass roots and gain a greater understanding of the demands of a camp.

Judy is also aware that heading up the camp and its team gave her her first experience of leadership at a relatively young age and it gave her a good foundation for future roles – inside and outside the church. Collaborative leadership was not talked about much back then, but it was how the team worked and has been an underlying principle for her ever since, alongside gratitude for those who will both pray and act!

Equine Nightlife

With his SU hat on Alan Martin organised an annual staff weekend for as many members of SU and their families as could be squeezed in. Somehow the Carter family managed to be invited to help despite not being staff members.

'We were sleeping in Old 1 (now replaced by the pool cabin) when we were awakened at about one or two in the morning by very heavy breathing,' Bill says. 'We were somewhat used to the odd pony snuffling around eating the grass at the base of the cabin, but this was different, more like how a dragon would sound, if there are any' dragons left in the Quantocks. We went out to investigate, only to discover a foal in the pool. We woke Douglas and Mary Gibson, discussed the matter, then called the police. They referred the call to the fire brigade, who arrived quite quickly, first the fire chief in his Land Rover and then the fire engine complete with blue flashing lights but thankfully no sirens. By the time the main crew had disembarked, the fire chief with Douglas had hauled the foal out of the pool. There then followed a fascinating twenty minutes or so while they carefully checked the foal over for injury, noted a small cut to its leg, established from the brand of the adult horses further up the field to whom it belonged and then released it back to its mother. The adult horses then chased it round the field four or five times in a circle to warm it up before heading out through the back gate and into the forest. We invited the firemen into the kitchen for tea and a chat before resuming our sleep. The next day we learned that only one other person had woken, and when she had told her husband that there was a blue flashing light in the field he had told her not to be silly and to go back to sleep!'

Trials of a Medical Officer

When Sylvia Fox was MO for the girls' camp, in the eighties, she had the original Old 10 as her base. 'One night I woke up to hear what sounded at least like a sheep, and more likely a horse or deer, apparently digging up the back corner. I got my wellies on and a torch and went out to investigate. I'm not sure who was more surprised – the *hedgehog* or me! It was making an immense noise for one so small.

'The scariest thing that happened was a potential spinal injury at one of the girls' camps. I was the junior MO (a not yet qualified physio at that stage), and staying calm whilst asking, 'Can you feel me touching your skin here?' was a growing-up moment for me. What I learnt from it has stayed with me for good: get on with it, and use your training, whilst asking God's strength at the same time. All was well in the end, but seeing a teenager being carried into the kitchen on an old mattress from the store in the JI hut was a bit like a clash of biblical stories and an A&E moment – except the 'stretcher' bearers were dressed in swim-shorts, and the one taking the calm lead (well, calm on the outside, even if he wasn't inside) was David Whitehouse.

'One of Margaret's girls' adventure camps ended up with the banquet at the end of camp being a full-scale Christmas meal with all the trimmings, and Mary Gibson made the Christmas puddings to bring with her. The tables were complete with paper chains and crackers and paper serviettes (all of which Mary had bought in the sale in January), and there was a decorated pine tree. The idea had begun from a chance comment when one of the planning team said, "I like Christmas pudding, but not at Christmas." Somehow that then morphed into the banquet being Christmas – and teaching that we can celebrate Christ's birth at any time of year. It's just fortunate no hikers came in asking for directions that night – they would have gone away with a pretty odd view of Scripture Union!

'A much more sombre time was when the local police force were searching the upper moors for murder clues following the discovery of a body, and they came to us for hot drinks and the use of the toilet, the link being, I think, that one of the policemen was a warden at St Mary's, Nether Stowey. We sent them up with a full biscuit tin and an urn of tea for the team of searchers.

'The whole of camp is something still hugely with me: the place where Sunday school Bible stories (greatly enjoyed) suddenly became personal. No one officer's teaching stands out; the lessons came from everyone – both in teaching and, far more, in actions.'

Sub Work Party

The kitchen is perhaps the room above all others at camp that sees most use. Vast quantities of steam are produced to condense on the ceiling. The greasy pots and pans are washed up there, the tea and coffee pots are emptied with inevitable splashing. So there is regular need to clean and redecorate it, especially the section of the ceiling above the water boiler, but the Easter work party is not the best time because the kitchen is needed to prepare hot food to keep the team going.

On at least two occasions the Carter family found themselves camping out in the mess hut in February or March in order that they could paint the kitchen out of season. 'Douglas Gibson on one of those visits disconnected the water boiler and moved it to the outside wash-up so that we had hot water without condensation dripping from the newly painted ceiling,' says Bill. 'I hesitate to say it, but I think it was so cold that time that we decided washing could wait until we got home. The work started early in the morning and continued until late at night to ensure that we completed the task, but my abiding memory, as well as the cold, was snuggling down in our sleeping bags (on mattresses) in front of the open fire in the mess hut and drifting off to sleep with the flickering fire for company.'

Bosun's Store

'Over the winter of 1983 to 1984 a new bosun's store was built,' Alan Martin writes. 'Storage had always been a problem, and the old bosun's store had become seriously inadequate for all the camping gear and bedding. Half of the new building now houses Great Wood SU camp equipment while the Somerset LEA uses the other half as an office-cum-store.'

'For those lovers of antiquity,' Bill Carter adds, 'the old bread bin has been rehoused there of late and now stores a miscellaneous collection of wellington boots left behind over the years at the end of camps. It is a pleasant reminder of those good old days when Wilf brought the bread up to the kitchen and then sat for a while chatting over a cup of tea.'

At the time of writing, the old bosun's store still stands, and houses various left-over building materials which 'might come in useful'.

Stones

Bill continues, 'Many and varied have been the attempts to drain the field. In 1984 it was decided to employ a firm to lay three land drains running diagonally from the chapel cabin to the swimming pool. Feeding into these was a complete herringbone network of side drains. These drains were at least eighteen inches down and the trenches backfilled with coarse grit before having some of the topsoil put back to "level" the field again. It doesn't take much imagination to picture the field after this work was completed. The trench-digging machinery had unearthed a lot of large stones. There were ridges all across the field and it was difficult to traverse it in the dark.

'When we arrived at the start of the work party we found that the LEA groups who had been in before us had, under Derek Briggs, made a huge start on collecting the large stones and there was a considerable pile of them between Cabin 6 and the entrance to the chapel. It was decided that these stones could be used to good effect to strengthen the bank of the stream at the other end of the field where, at the time, the climbing rope/swing hung. Having moved two or three wheelbarrow loads it was agreed that it would take longer than we had to complete the task in this manner. Peter Hudson, with his usual resourcefulness, had noted that a man with a JCB was staying at Adscombe Farm. I believe that they were acquainted with one another but I didn't know that at the time. The next thing I knew was that a large yellow JCB was trundling across the field and with barely any effort had scooped up the entire pile, transported it to the other end of the field and spread it out.'

A Lifetime of Memories Continues

In 1981 another new camp was invented. Gill Hollis attended In Take for 17s–25s from 1981 to 1984. 'Led by Anton Baumohl, we seemed to spend a good deal of time sitting around chatting, or doing very odd challenges, or dancing "I Want to Be Near You (you're the one, the one, the one)" in a variety of locations including Exmoor in the rain and Taunton station as we waited for the train home. On one occasion we had to choose from a list of items to carry with us on a series of challenges over the Quantocks (which included carrying one of the team on a stretcher which we had to construct en route). We didn't know what might or might not be needed, so the choice was purely at random. I still don't know why we chose the plunger, but I brandished it triumphantly as we carried it across the finish line to win the challenge.

'In 1982 I became a junior officer for the first time. Half of my time had to be spent in the kitchen (with the same people who had passed plates under the table and fed me toast at midnight). My main memory of this is being asked to empty the teabags out of the teapots. I didn't have the courage to tell the cooks that the smell of tea makes me feel queasy, so I just had to try to grin and bear it. But I loved being with the girls in the cabin. Some of them had older sisters my age, so we spent a lot of time just sitting chatting.

'Another year I was awoken from my slumbers in the JI hut by Clare Nichols asking if I had a camper in the room with me. One of my cabin had gone missing. She had seemed rather reluctant to leave the grandparents who had brought her the day before. I remembered that they were staying in a caravan in Spaxton. Gerry Nichols drove over there in the middle of the night and, sure enough, there she was. How she had managed to get herself there we will never know. But thank God she was safe! She didn't return to camp … but she and her grandparents did come to Nether Stowey church on Sunday (she looked sheepish, they looked embarrassed).

'And the day we had an officer hunt in Burnham-on-Sea will forever be remembered. One member of the team spent the day as a mechanic under a car so no one found him; Graham Brown hid in a bin liner on the prom and startled passers-by; the two who were window cleaners almost got themselves arrested for unsolicited window cleaning. I staggered about in a wig and Mary Gibson's shoes, dressed as an old lady. And Angela Doughty, dressed as a scout leader, was accosted by a man from the local mission who asked her, "Do you know the Lord?" to which she replied, "Lord who?"

'I remained a member of the team at various camps until 1998. It was as a leader at the girls' camp that I first led an evening meeting, well trained by Angela and Ruth Gibson (now Mason). Dawn Hilton (now Brown) and I took over the evening leading (which I loved ... perhaps this was the start of my lay reader training?) and I wrote four or five play scripts that we used as the basis for the camp theme ... on board a ship, in the jungle, in an office where the cleaner (played so magnificently by Dawn) could smell trouble. Those ten days of August were some of the happiest days of my summer, especially the year when I was the sole cabin officer for Cabin 3 and we won the cabin competition. (Oh, the fun every evening of putting the points up on the board on the wall in the corner!)

'And cabin inspections – what a joy! And the year that each cabin decided to have a theme for their inspection, until one cabin had "rubbish tip" as their theme, at which point Ruth Gibson had to ban themed inspections!

'I went to the work party for the first time in 1988. How odd to be working with people who had known me as a camper at the age of twelve. But the smell of creosote was so beautiful (how sad that it is no longer allowed to be used).

'1989 was a momentous year at work party ... into the mess hut on the first evening walked a man in a suit who was on a project building the new Convention Centre in Birmingham. Peter and I were married in August 1990 (after the girls' camp, of course). In 1992 we brought our two-and-a-half-week-old baby to work party. We think she was the youngest ever camper.

'And here we still are twenty-six years on. That tiny baby is now wearing her dad's old boiler suit and wood-preserving the cabins while I paint and Peter still makes and mends.'

Alone with God

One anonymous member of Chris Owen's team remembers 'going on a night walk one of my first years at a Great Wood camp, a proper night walk when it was already dark, we weren't allowed any torches and were advised to wear very sturdy footwear. We scrambled up steep inclines that would be difficult even with the full sun shining down, which was fun and scary, but also took time for a prayer walk in the dark. We all separated out, so that no one was walking together, and then we had to walk a distance alone along a wide clear track. The idea was to have some space without distraction from other people, from noise, from the surrounding views, to be free to think or pray. It was a little tense because you literally could not see anything except for the light-stoned path ahead and the outlines of the vegetation at our sides, not knowing what was there or not there, but it was also immensely peaceful. I don't remember praying or thinking about anything in particular, but I still look back on that night and think of Great Wood being a place where we can find peace and calm, despite the craziness of the rest of camp!'

Teaching Backwoodsman Skills

'Anyone who has been through Scouts or Cadet Force will remember many things they have learnt,' Mike Menzies says. 'But have they been useful in later life? I was taught how to use an axe, the safety considerations, the technique etc. But in my later life I realised that different instruments were needed for different situations. So I introduced the bow saw and felling axe into the axemanship training.

'All of the tools require practice to improve skills. But the felling axe also requires strength, so, having proved skill with an axe, I required the camper merely to demonstrate sufficient strength. I held the axe at arm's length and found I could hold it for about fifteen seconds. I considered myself proficient with the felling axe, and so the ten-second test was born. Several campers passed the test.

'When the rules require a campsite cooking stove to be lit with no more than two matches, the kindling must be good. Though I put in time and effort to collect suitable kindling, one has to demonstrate the fire-lighting without failure. Drying the kindling in the oven may come as a surprise to the kitchen staff, and may be considered cheating by outdoor staff, but life is too short for perfection.'

Joel Carter too has memories of making sure. 'In my case, when the weather turned I found myself with an old towel and a hairdryer, attempting to dry a small branch for the axemanship demonstration.'

Wildlife

Jenny Hudson's son Michael, when he was about two, had a Fisher-Price pull-along tortoise and was outside pulling it up and down the path to the JI hut. Jenny was in the kitchen when a camper came to the door and said Michael had a tortoise.

'Yes, I know.'

'No, Michael has a tortoise.'

'Yes, a pull-along one.'

'*No*, Michael has a tortoise, a real one.'

'Sure enough,' Jenny says now, 'he was walking down the path with a large, very much alive tortoise. We brought it back to Yorkshire to give it a home and named it GW. But it was an escapologist. After the second try we never saw it again.

'On another occasion a few years later we went to Tropiquaria, to the reptile house. I lost my daughter Charlotte – nothing new there – but as I came around the corner there she was with a python draped around her neck!

'About once each camp the cooks managed to get out for a break. We were having a cream tea at the Castle Café in Nether Stowey when Peter Hudson gate-crashed. He had not seen a cafetière before and before we could stop him he said, "What's this for?" and pushed the plunger down. The contents exploded all over the teas, which rather took the edge off the outing.'

Elizabeth Carter remembers the cooks' afternoon tea out. 'It was a regular feature in the 1980s when we had ten-day camps and was a valuable way to say thank you to the cooks for the important job they do at camp. We often take for granted the absence of gastroenteritis in camp, but this is thanks a lot to the efforts of cooks in sometimes challenging circumstances. Perhaps the best example would be when Liz Lauste (now Hollis) came to an Easter camp in 1975 unknowingly carrying typhoid and not a single person on the camp became ill!'

End of an Era

'One of the remaining landmarks of early Great Wood, Old 10, was consigned to the flames at the Youth Focus camp in 1990,' Alan Martin says. 'Age had taken its toll and it was uncertain quite what was holding it up. In its place (not exactly risen from the ashes) is a

Old 10

fine New 10 (now known as the chapel cabin), a stretched version of the main cabins providing two double bedrooms for staff and a small central room for group work.'

New 10, also known as the chapel cabin

1990s: From Generation to Generation

A Parent's Perspective from Ruth Nicholls

'Sue Keighley and her husband Andrew ran the young adults' camp SPACE from 1995 to 2013. Her children have been at Great Wood since before they were born, and all of them are involved with current activities there. Sue is now a trustee and Lucy keeps us updated with camp news so that we are able to pray regularly for all that is happening at camp.

'The contribution which the activities at Great Wood have made to our family is a constant source of thanks to the Lord Jesus. We have watched with joy the impact that sound Christian teaching and fun and fellowship with friends has had on the campers' maturing in the Faith. Our gratitude for the work done at Great Wood over many years is enormous and it is our prayer that the Lord will continue to use that lovely place for the growth of His kingdom.'

A Parent's Lack of Perspective

In 1991, as leaders of the Backwoodsman camp, Bill and Elizabeth Carter took all the boys to Nether Stowey church on Sunday. 'Afterwards,' Bill says, 'we checked that all the boys were either walking back with the walking group or had gone by car before we ourselves left. We arrived back at camp and had set about getting ready for Sunday lunch when we were interrupted by a phone call. It was a lady from Nether Stowey church.

'"Have you left one of your campers at church?"

'"No, I don't think so. They are all accounted for."

'"Well, we have a young girl here that we don't recognise who says she is from Great Wood Camp."

'In our concern to account for all the campers we had failed to remember our daughter Lydia. She was apparently unconcerned about being left behind, assuring the worried parishioners that we would be back! I dread to think how long it would have been before we realised.'

Out of the Mouths

Steve and Judy Hutchinson, leaders and SU workers, remember, 'Our young son, after his first visit to Great Wood (for a staff weekend), in a conversation about what heaven would be like, said, "I think it will be like Great Wood." We also have a lovely picture of him later, aged seven, learning to ride without stabilisers down the middle of the field and being very excited about it.

'The communion service in the outdoor chapel at the staff weekends was always very special and included all ages contributing and also taking communion. It was the first place where our young children were invited to take part.'

Catching the Vision and Passing It On

'One thread runs strong through my years of Great Wood: the thread of community,' says the Rev. Chris Owen, camper and leader from the 1970s. 'As a child, I remember the first time I was allowed to be part of a work team at the annual work party. I was probably more hindrance than help, but was constantly supported and helped as I learned the ropes. We downed tools together, ending the day muddy, exhausted and satisfied at a hole well dug, and a job well done.

'And then the community of campers, a gang of eight boys with no connection before arriving in the same cabin, telling jokes after lights out until we were laughing too loud and were told off by a rampaging leader. Laughing so much on orienteering that we fell off the path and rolled down a heather-covered hill. Stilling ourselves to listen to the stories about the love of Jesus. Basking in the light of a last-night camp fire that seemed to touch the sky. Friendships forged with light and laughter that have lasted decades.

'Too old to be a camper, and it's time to learn to lead. Stepping behind the curtain and seeing the prayer, effort, energy and passion that are thrown into the mix of a team. Putting the brakes on a game that is going too fast, cleaning plates after everyone else has gone off to a meeting, sharing heart and soul when it's time to talk. Walking in awe of the experienced old hands, and basking in their praise and encouragement at my toddler steps into leadership.

Handing over leadership of a team

83

'And then looking around, and realising that I'm the old hand, and that it's my turn to dish out encouragement and praise. Spotting the gifts in those making those tentative first steps. Knowing who to slow down and who to boost, who to drive harder and who to give rest. And watching friendships grow deep and deeper and bonds form that will last decades.

'The community of friends that meet with a purpose and a plan, that purpose and plan which is to be a community gathered around the person of Jesus.'

Alice's Broken Wrist

'It was 1990 or 1991, I think (what? You expect me to remember dates as well?), and Alice, my daughter, would have been five or six,' writes Ed Wicke, part of the work party team. 'I'd had a book published by Kingsway, and was in the habit of telling stories to children. So after supper a little gang, ages four to twelve I guess, gathered in one of the cabins and perched on the bunk beds. I can't recall which stories I told – possibly "Mouldysocks" or "Alicroc the Alien". There was a lot of laughter. And then, foolishly, I tried another . . .

'Alice decided to walk along the bunk rails. She recalls that she'd already been warned not to do this, but she was getting bored (she'd heard all the stories many times). And maybe the sugar rush from the Easter chocolate was partly to blame for her restlessness! She leaned out too far . . . tumbled . . . landed on her left wrist . . . broke it . . . and cried out. The session was being taped and I played back the recording only once before binning it, because that cry of pain was too hard to listen to.

'We all felt pretty bad about this, and Alice was in a lot of pain. But she returned from her speedy trip to hospital with a wrist cast she was rather proud of, and it absorbed its share of Great Wood mud and autographs before we went home a day or two later.

'The Great Wood Emergency Response Mode should be legendary in its own right. I recall that people mobilised instantly and Alice was being driven off within minutes; the distraught storyteller was hugged and given hot chocolate (there wouldn't have been so much as a thimbleful of wine in the camp back then), and all children were quickly bundled off to bed with promises that Alice would be fine. I also recall that Pauline Whitehouse was so moved to pity that she sat down and wrote a little story for Alice to read the next day.'

A Pool Cabin Is Born

With Old 10 gone the oldest remaining building was Old 1, Bill Carter remembers. Over the winter of 1990 to 1991 Old 1 was taken down (with a vague idea of re-erecting it to the left of the main gate) and in its place a cabin, very similar in design to New 10, was constructed. This provided much more comfortable accommodation for team members and, with the sleeping quarters divided into two separate rooms, allowed more privacy for married couples.

The Funnies

'Bizarrely, as a camper the first thing I can remember is meeting "Duvet" in all his delightful eccentricity as he strolled around the cabins poking his head in,' Paul Vines says. (Duvet was a teenager who turned up at Easter camp without a sleeping bag. When he demanded a duvet, the nickname stuck!) 'Many of my favourite times were in our Youth Focus (as it was then) Thrash Out groups. I loved the combination of sharing some great laughs and talking about deep things. I have particularly fond memories of my year in Rich Clarke's group and my year with Roger Widdecombe and Mary Scott.

'Obviously I loved the talks and singing. Coming from a fairly dull village church it was amazing to sing fun, dynamic songs and listen to engaging talks.

'The evenings were often my favourite time. Country dancing and then a Winnie-the-Pooh story with different voices read by Neil Nicholls by the fire. Back to our cabins to discuss the day and catch up on which girls we liked into the small hours.

'After a year off I couldn't help but want to go back as a leader. I loved investing in young people's lives in the same way that people had invested in me.

'I remember being asked to help with the Funnies by Matt Loe, Jono Owens, Marshy and Chris Owen. They told me it was our job to help people relax a bit and laugh. We'd often stay up really late writing the most ridiculous scripts and thinking of tag lines that we would get the whole camp saying. "How about that?" "Can't see it from my house." "What a guy!" We came up with ridiculous stories like "The Knights of the Picnic Table", "The Brian, the Titch and the Wardrobe" and "The Legend of Captain Camp", about Captain Camp's quest to find Captain Camper. There was Matt Loe in the role of Fiona (sniff) Ipswich and the silly titles we gave the news. We even introduced the start-of-the-day Bible studies as a load of Prayer And New Testament Studies! All that's just to name a few.

'For some reason it was decided that Jan Simmons should check the scripts to make sure they were appropriate. I was chosen to show them to her each day. We'll leave how some of the more edgy jokes got through to Great Wood folklore!

'Great Wood will always have a special place in my life. It is where I became a Christian after talking with Rich Clarke for hours one afternoon on a walk. It is where I made lifelong friends. It is where I saw that being a Christian could also be really fun. It is where I laughed, cried, sang, danced, blushed, showered most, breathed deepest and came alive.'

John Simmons testifies that Paul held the camp record in those days for the most showers: thirteen in a six-day camp!

A New Broom

John Owen will never forget being asked by Bill and Elizabeth Carter if he would be interested in taking the Backwoodsman camp on from them when they stepped down. 'To be asked was a huge privilege. Many, I know, are daunted by the prospect, but I seemed to be conveniently oblivious to any potential difficulties, despite having been on the team for the previous ten years!

'The first hurdle was being approved as a leader by SU. I have never had such a grilling, where I felt that both my ability to lead and the relevance of an all-boys camp with "traditional" activities were being heavily challenged.

'It was exciting and a relief to be approved as the leader and able to set the wheels in motion and start getting a team together. Thankfully many good people from previous years were happy to come back, and I remember having great fun bouncing ideas off my dad and having lengthy phone conversations and impromptu planning weekends with my core team. This all culminated in a very intensive official planning weekend, where we seemed to work non-stop from Friday evening to Sunday afternoon.

'The month before camp, every spare moment in an incredibly busy work time was taken up with some kind of planning. The camp itself was ten days of emotional extremes as I was determined that everything would work, and work perfectly. I did far too much micro-managing and triple-checking. There were probably moments I was not very bearable. Nevertheless it all seemed to go well. After camp I was exhausted, until about March the next year.

'Leading a camp has very high and very low moments, moments of great joy and moments of great tension, moments of rush and pressure and moments of sitting back watching it all happen. I generally found I could ride most of that, but as the years went by I found the pre- and particularly post-camp admin more and more tedious.

'Answers to prayer are a real high. One year we had a major team crisis. Not only were we short on team numbers but we were severely lacking in many key areas. A few days before camp I had a letter from the father of a boy booked in. He was trying in vain to persuade his son to go. The only hope was if his dad could come; was there space for another helper? The dad in question was Andrew Downing, who had had plenty of experience at Great Wood. I tried not to sound too desperate in saying, "Yes, please." He ended up helping me out for a few years with his wife Jane, and then went on to take over from me leading the camp. But that year, his presence and input made a huge difference, possibly even in making the camp viable.

'There are far too many funny incidents to mention. There was the constant wit and banter of the team, the regular practical jokes and the spectacular things which went wrong in a no-harm-done sort of way. Thankfully, we never had any really serious accidents or incidents.

'Over the fifteen years I ran the camp much changed, including the name – to GWX. I like to think I became more concerned with serving the boys who came on the camp and less concerned with the detail of the programme, more concerned with meeting people where they were and less with the number of "converts", more interested in having time just to "be" and less in having a relentless programme, and I hope, more gracious and less irascible. On the other hand, after fifteen years I was starting to lose the raw enthusiasm, and it was time to let someone else step in.

'I am indebted to a very large number of people: highly competent and willing team members who just got on with what needed doing; people both in and out of camp who gave me a huge amount of personal support; two top-class caterers who produced perfect meals for energetic adults and children in abundant quantities.

'I will treasure in my mind moments sitting on a bench on the now-gone mess hut patio looking out across the field, groups of boys and leaders gathered round small fires, others playing in the stream, others playing football, others running around in groups playing games, or quietly practising knots, reading or whatever else. Chatter, occasional laughter, occasional friendly shouts. People getting on together, helping each other, making lifelong friends. That was, to me, where the presence of God was very real.'

Space: the Final Something

'Andy and I ran Space camps between 1995 and 2013,' Sue Keighley writes. 'We had been involved with lots of other camps at Great Wood before this, notably Youth Focus, which had an upper age limit of seventeen. At the time, Scripture Union had only one camp for the eighteen-plus age range; this was called Growth into Leadership. There was no Soul Survivor or Momentum back then. We saw time after time young people coming through the camps at Great Wood and then having limited options after the age of seventeen. Not all of them wanted to grow into leadership, or certainly not immediately.

'The vision for Space was to provide the best possible Christian holiday for the eighteen-plus age range. The aim was to provide a happy, welcoming, helpful and encouraging environment where people could come even if they weren't sure where they were on their Christian journey and could bring their non-Christian friends. It was an enormous joy to have the opportunity to develop something from scratch and to have such freedom for creativity. We had a fantastic team to work with and together we had a lot of fun planning each event and bringing it to fruition.

'Often there would be a theme for the camp – a particular favourite of mine was "Greece" (Chris Owen running down the hillside in a toga with a flaming torch to the music from *Chariots of Fire* was particularly memorable!). We would plan and build stage props for the week – anything from very large paddling pools with golden (play safe) sand surround to rockets crash-landing into the mess hut roof – and one year had a full-blown Christmas as our last-night hurrah. Turkey and all the trimmings. Finding a suitable Christmas tree wasn't too much of a challenge!

'The lighting of the camp fire became a year-long planning challenge for a small posse of the team. Ever more entertaining or elaborate schemes were put into place.

'We wanted every single camper to feel valued and treasured. We would invest in lovely soaps, shower gel, other fun toiletries, new shower curtains in the days of the shower blocks, and also wanted the food and logistics to be top-notch.

'One very special year was 2001 – the year of the foot and mouth outbreak. The Quantocks, along with the rest of the countryside, had been on lockdown, but we had been hoping that things would reopen in time for Space. About ten days before camp was due to start we were told that the countryside ban would not be lifted and so, with heavy hearts, we cancelled Space. Some people made other plans. Then, a couple of days before camp was supposed to start, the ban was lifted. We quickly rang around and rallied about half of the team and campers. It was a little bit like rediscovering Sleeping Beauty's castle. No one had been into the Quantocks or on site for months. It was verdant and peaceful and beautiful. Because of the reduced number of people, the only way that it could work was for everyone to muck in. We adopted a "seamless" approach to running the camp: team and non-team alike had a role to play in making things happen, although the team had been praying and preparing in advance. And this seamless ethos became a big part of Space thereafter.

'The worship and teaching were high-priority. We started Praise Up, a pre-breakfast time of worship and reflection. This gave people the chance to spend more time in what would in today's Christian lingo be called "soaking" than there was room for in the main sessions. Many of the teaching series had a lasting impact. One year the theme of camp was SMILE and the titles of the five talks across the week began with the five letters. Personally, the I for "Intentional Living" has been an important and meaningful message.

'As well as the worship and teaching, the sessions always had an element of fun. "The Funnies" were extraordinary! From Chief Honolulu to Gross Habit, the Naked Chef, the Blue Man, the Spice Girls, Wellness and some slick film editing with live action from Matt and Jono which paved the way for Take That ... many a chuckle. Also lots of entertainments around the camp fire with the regular last-night feature of "The Twelve Days of Space Camp", a round-up of what had happened during our time at camp.

'We were very aware that the campers, or non-team, were at a transitional stage of life – finishing school, moving to university, starting first jobs – and we wanted to encourage them and help to prepare them for some of the challenges of life. Every Space we would run a variety of workshops. These covered budgeting, hygiene and skin care, cooking healthily on a low income, an overview of the Bible, media awareness, mental health, environmental awareness and sustainable living – to name but a few.

'There were dawn walks, *Charlie and the Chocolate Factory* (an AA man frightened on being greeted in the middle of the forest by a couple of Oompa Loompas), wild water swimming on Exmoor, cream teas at various lovely tea rooms, picnics at Kilve, star gazing, camel treks (yes, really), pizzas at Suzie's, cinema trips, fish and chips and lots of ice cream.

'Running Space was a privilege and a joy, but seeing the major and ongoing work of the Holy Spirit in people's lives and knowing it began at camp is even better! We praise the Lord for every encounter and pray that He will continue to move and grow in people's lives.

'The team were great and there are too many to mention everyone, but some people really went the distance with us and were involved over many years. We would like to acknowledge and thank them: Jim and Mary Rennison, Nick Weaver, Andy

Batterham, Jono and Anne Owen, Claire and James Aston, Roger and Hannah Widdecombe, and Harry Carr. We couldn't have done it without you.

'I leave you with a picture from the first ever Space: on the last night we are all gathered under a beautiful, starlit sky listening to an unplugged session from Iain Archer, "Wishing". When I contacted Iain to ask if he could come to play at the tenth Space his agent came back to say that he loved Space and would have really liked to do it, but he was on tour with Snow Patrol.

'Thank you, Lord, for such happy, special Space camps.'

Bowing to the Inevitable

In 1996 mains water came to Great Wood. A number of traditionalists, Bill Carter included, thought that this was giving in to city softies, but in reality it was bowing to the inevitable. The water supply feeding Great Wood from the spring up the combe was still flowing, but the increasing use of the hills for recreation as well as the ongoing agricultural work meant that in times of heavy rain, chemicals were being leached out of the soil and finding their way into the supply. There had been a number of cases of sickness spoiling Youth Focus and it was thought that the water supply could be a contributing factor. To mollify the old guard the tap in the passageway by the staff toilet was left connected to the old system. This had the obvious benefit of allowing access to fresh water even if the rest of the system had been shut off to drain it down for maintenance. The bulk of the water now comes from the local Hawkridge Reservoir, being cleaned at Ashford treatment works before being pumped to a holding reservoir on the hillside behind camp.

Another Wedding at Great Wood

From Ed Wicke's Christmas letter of 1998:

'Rachel ... is married! The Dream Wedding happened at Great Wood Camp, on about the only sunny day this summer – ruining all my plans for a huge mudfight during the ceremony (one has to keep up the Great Wood traditions). We had also speculated about the possibility of having the aerial runway put up early so that she could glide down it and land gracefully at the old wooden cross, attired in white lace and black wellingtons. In the end we paraded sedately across the field to music from *Star Trek – The Movie*. I had to hobble down the aisle to give Rachel away because I'd been playing at the stream the day before, slipped and sprained my ankle, to the amusement of many.

'It was a wonderful time for all of us, starting the day before when a wedding work party turned up & set to, and ending with the ritual Great Wood tidy-up the day after. Unfortunately, Rachel & husband Steve (Eggington) couldn't stay for the cleaning part but had to go on honeymoon in Cornwall instead ...'

2000s: Luxury Comes to Great Wood

⸻ ❦ ⸻

Changes occurred when the Great Wood Estate Group (GWEG) was set up to manage the site on the retirement of Alan Martin. SU delegated to this group the oversight of the site, its maintenance and care. John Simmons, who chaired GWEG, takes up the story:

Beginning of GWEG

In 2000, GWEG discussed with Scripture Union the possibility of the appointment of a schools worker to work specifically with the schools that use Great Wood. GWEG believed it would be possible to fund this post in part from surpluses arising from the management of the estate, and in part from team support, mainly from the large number of people who knew and loved the place. This tied in with a review at Scripture Union. Like every other Christian organisation (indeed, every Christian!), SU was feeling a need to ensure every financial commitment was in line with exactly what God wanted done. Resources were precious and needed to be fully utilised.

Lesley Blight reflects that the work at Great Wood obviously had been greatly blessed, with many stories of God at work through a programme of residential events during school holidays. 'For a large part of the year, though, the site was let for use by Kilve Court, a nearby residential centre used by the Somerset Local Education Authority to provide residential experience for school pupils as part of their curriculum. It was of course a great help financially to have the regular letting, and undoubtedly the

94

children would have valued being in such a beautiful place. But could more be done to fulfil Scripture Union and Great Wood's shared aim of making Jesus known? Could new opportunities be found to extend ministry?

'It was decided to appoint a field worker to the south-west team who could have a specific focus in developing ministry at Great Wood, including offering to work with Kilve and the local authority to introduce a spiritual aspect to the term-time work. Caroline Armstrong was appointed in 2001 with a remit to help establish a greater understanding of Great Wood's Christian heritage and ethos and to offer activities to school groups, including collective worship, in line with legal educational requirements.'

Caroline started to build relationships with the management at Kilve. It quickly became apparent that achieving our desire of getting a greater Christian influence into Great Wood during term time was not going to be easy. Her experience was in stark contrast with that of many of SU's schools workers, who are often warmly welcomed by school authorities.

This experience made the trustees realise that, if we were to achieve a greater Christian influence on site, we had to be in a position to negotiate changes to the LEA licence agreement from a position of strength. In turn this meant being prepared to go it alone, without the benefit of their licence fee, marketing and special relationship with Somerset schools. Our preferred route was to co-operate with Kilve. So we started to take advice from others who run similar Christian centres without any special links with a LEA, and from teachers who are responsible for choosing venues for outdoor education courses.

It quickly became clear to us that, although Great Wood had been well maintained and lovingly cared for over the years, the facilities were now way behind modern standards. In particular, the toilet arrangements and the difficulty of night-time supervision were two major problems, both from a child protection viewpoint and in terms of modern expectations of comfort. The pool was nearing the end of its useful life and would also need rebuilding to a modern specification, with the inclusion of a heating system, if it was to be used for school children.

It is interesting to note how long it took us to get to a radical solution! For some months we toyed with the idea of building an extension onto each of the existing cabins, to provide a loo, hand basin and shower. We had these designed and 'Gilbert costed', and discussed the concept with planners. Gilbert costing was itself an art form. Gilbert Villis had for some years done most of the major building work at Great Wood, and knew where every pipe and land drain ran. He had joined with volunteers in giving the place the loving care which has been such a feature of Great Wood for so long. He worked on an hourly charge basis, and only had a very hazy idea as to how long it would take to build something. He built each of the 'stretched' cabins, the final cost of which varied considerably even though each was basically the same design. He was, however, an invaluable resource for building work which was beyond the scope of the annual work party.

A vision began to emerge of a Christian education centre, staffed with Christians, into which schools would bring their children during term time for curriculum-based activities, and which, because of the excellence of its facilities, the splendid location and the attitude of its staff, would be a preferred location for many schools. A centre which would continue with the SU camping tradition in holiday time, but would also be able to offer weekends to church groups during term time, and half-term short breaks for families and other groups. A centre where SU would control what went on, whilst honouring any contract terms which might be agreed with Kilve or with Somerset LEA. A site to which gap year students could come to provide young, enthusiastic Christian role models for school-aged kids.

From this larger picture came the realisation that we would be foolish to spend substantial amounts of money on alterations to cabins that were already nearly forty years old, and the idea grew that we should think big and design a new cabin suitable for the next forty to fifty years. In this we were fortunate to be able to call on the expertise and enthusiasm of Michael Phillips, who had designed the mess hut and then-existing cabins. The brief given to Michael was to design a cabin for eight children, with a separate room for leaders or teachers (thus replacing the sleeping boxes in the four corners of the JI hut) and with its own washing and showering facilities, in such a way as to be visually in sympathy with the site.

With Michael, we met on site with the planners, who were surprisingly positive about our ideas, stressing the importance of visual impact and of limiting total numbers accommodated. In fact, all the way through the planning process we had no opposition from either the planners or the local council – evidence, I am sure, of the power of prayer to enable something which is in line with the Lord's will to happen.

Whilst the design for the new cabins was being worked on we got on with the more straightforward task of adding a toilet and shower to the relatively new 'stretched' cabins. Incorporated in these plans were disabled access to one of the cabins, and a design which would make the pool cabin suitable to house three gap year students for the summer. The work of providing services to all the cabins was incorporated into these plans, which were carried out by Gilbert over the winters of 2001/02 and 2002/03. Old SU hands couldn't get over the luxury of team member accommodation with all mod cons!

During 2002 we worked with Michael on plans for the new cabins, and eventually had a design that we could discuss with potential suppliers of prefabricated wooden buildings. Building six new cabins within the closed period of a winter (November to March) was clearly beyond Gilbert's capacity, and we knew we had to get the timing of the build programme planned carefully in advance, laying the foundations before mud and frost took over.

We located three suppliers who were able and willing to manufacture to our own design, and, after visits to sites to see the results of their handiwork, and indicative prices, we chose a Canadian company. They explained that they would build a cabin, roofed in and with windows and external doors fitted, in around two weeks, and would leave us to fit out the interiors and do the plumbing and electrical work. Gerry Nichols did some detailed calculations on the work which would fall to us, and estimated seven weeks per cabin, given a reasonable amount of volunteer labour.

We agreed that the suppliers would organise the construction in such a way that they would hand over to us a cabin a week, starting mid-January. This would enable us to get all cabins completed before Storm went in on 2nd April – tight, but possible. The foundations were laid in good time before Christmas. Lynch & Co, who did the work, were efficient and timely, covering minor variations in specification within their original quote. Careful preparation and specifying by Michael and Gerry meant a job done well and on time.

Meanwhile, Michael had worked up detailed plans with the suppliers, ready for submission for planning and building regulations approval. A combination of careful preparation and full explanation led to a trouble-free passage through the planning process, which we took as God's seal of approval on the enterprise.

SU helped us with the financial aspect of our plans by taking Caroline onto the SU independent schools' budget with effect from April 2003, which enabled GWEG to make a sizable annual contribution to the cost of the development. They encouraged us to include everything that we anticipated would need attention in the development costings, including refurbishing the JI hut, minor alterations to the mess hut consequent on the removal of washing facilities, and the replacement of the swimming pool.

What we failed to take into consideration was the likelihood that our sewage disposal system would need major attention. Gilbert

Architect Michael Phillips inspecting progress

had kept it going faithfully for many years, but we discovered during the planning process that there was no evidence of there being any permission for it, and it discharged directly into the stream! Even though at that time it was working well, and was not causing any discharge problems, we needed later to include an amount of £35,000 in our spending plans to install a bio-digester in order to be safe in this area.

With the estimated cost of the cabins, the whole project came to £357,000, to which SU agreed a grant of £160,000. With a realistic annual contribution over five years from our own estate resources, this left £157,000 to raise by appeal.

Having got this far, I sought the advice of a longstanding supporter of Great Wood, Horace Webber, who was the first person to lead a camp at Great Wood in John Inchley's time! He advised that we should first raise some money from close friends, going public with an appeal when we had a meaningful amount in hand. This was good advice, and, when we launched the appeal in 2003 we already had more than £60,000 in the kitty. With a grant of £20,000 from a trust for the bio-digester, we raised over £225,000 on the appeal, which enabled us to cope with additional costs on the cabins, and a higher specification for the pool caused by new regulations. Again, the financial story has been one of God's good provisions, as He has given us the right amount to do the work we believe He is calling us to do. Not too much, as otherwise someone might feel their generosity was not needed. And not too little, so we were never tempted to cut corners, and do a job unworthy of the Kingdom of Heaven!

And so we were ready for the great adventure! There were many folk who came to help as volunteers from time to time, but I, John, would especially like to record thanks to:

- Andy Bennett, who had been my adjutant in days past, and who was in the process of being invalided out of the police force. He has since set up as 'the original Handy Andy', and was central to our ability to achieve all that we did internally. Subsequently he became our estate manager, taking over from Gerry Nichols, a post he still holds.
- David and Valerie Hornsby, who had recently returned from a three-year stint volunteering for SU Romania, and who were prepared to come and live in the Banda for several weeks, laying floors etc.
- Gerry Nichols, who kept us supplied with materials, did some of the complicated joinery bits, and entertained us with many erudite jokes.
- David Whitehouse, who organised a special February half-term work party, and who assembled a superb crew to give us a shot in the arm (and the odd TARDIS) just when we most needed it. Of his crew special mention of Peter Hollis, whose expertise on ceiling construction was of huge value, and who spared a further weekend when things were getting just a little bit tight!

Having given up his half-term, David went on to do another work party at Easter!

- Elizabeth Carter, who not only cooked for the work party, but also did a massive amount of stocking of the freezer, which kept the troops fed all through March and was a huge blessing at the end of a long day.
- Mike Menzies, who seemingly single-handed built patios and paths.
- Johnny Owen, who never lost faith in the belief that the Lord wanted us to deliver a usable campsite to the Easter teenage camp, now named Storm, who used his influence at Pip n Jay's in Bristol to get a gang from time to time, and who cheerfully came down himself from Bristol day after day to join in the fun.
- John Horton, a Great Wood camper from years ago, recently back from working for Tear Fund in Africa, who tirelessly looked after the field, clearing it of all manner of rubbish regardless of the weather conditions.
- My wife Jan, who contributed a huge amount to the planning process all through the programme, being in charge of all the furnishing and equipping of the cabins (within budget!) and joining in the manual work whenever she could escape from her real work! She did her best to limit the damage to the field, joining John Horton in repairing and tending wherever the Canadians would allow, and, above all, offered encouragement and a God-given conviction that we were facing an uphill spiritual battle which would be won at Eastertime.
- … and many others, whose input encouraged us on site, time and again, and without whose efforts we would never have been able to welcome Storm to a site where it was possible to run a camp.

By New Year 2004, four of the foundations were in, and the old cabins had been shipped down to a Christian campsite in Essex (where Gilbert disappeared for a week to reassemble them – only

Cabin 3 on the move

he knew how!). This was an answer to prayer. We had allowed for a cost of disposing of the old cabins, but I had secretly hoped some of the likely lads might take them away for use in back gardens. We made it known that they were available, with the proviso that if any other Christian organisation could use them, they would have first refusal. Nether Stowey PCC earmarked one. Then along came Ivan from the Essex Christian Fellowship, which was starting a tradition of Christian camping on his farm. SU agreed to give them to him on the basis that he paid for the transport costs – and they disappeared off site on 6th November, flat packed, to continue use in the Kingdom. Praise the Lord!

By 14th January, Lynch had finished laying all six bases, but there was no sign of the first container from Canada. Our suppliers had advised us that each cabin would arrive in its own container, and that these were scheduled to arrive at approximately weekly intervals. The first container eventually arrived on 26th January, with walls and roofs for two cabins, but no windows! The Canadian foreman, Charles, got the gang working on erecting the first two cabins, and, for a time, good progress was made. However, the second container with the windows in it didn't arrive until the 6th February and we were not given access to the first cabin for completion until the 11th, seven weeks before Storm were due to arrive.

Great Wood mud gets everywhere! The Canadians had purloined every patch of good grass we would allow them, but despite this the logs were distinctly muddy and had first to be scrubbed down inside before we started work on construction. Jan led a band of enthusiastic helpers, with Valerie and later Alison as valiant companions.

Normally the Easter camps at Great Wood have been difficult to fill, and we were pretty sure they would not need all six cabins, so at this point we were not too concerned. We just had to accelerate Gerry's seven-week fitting-out programme a bit! Provided we were given a cabin a week from this point on, we should be able to provide Storm with at least four cabins, and, as each held ten people, we reckoned this would be OK.

One of the Storm leaders, Chris Westlake, began to visit, advising us that this year Storm was absolutely full! Confidence still brimmed, and as yet we hadn't seen the spiritual battle which was looming. Yes, we prayed about the programme; yes, we asked the Lord's blessing on our activities, but we were not at the stage of crying out to the Lord for help.

By 16th February, the second cabin was ready for our attention, just in time for the half-term work party. This meant we made really good progress on these two, which began quickly to take shape inside.

Construction was complicated by two factors. First, logs shrink as they mature, and lose around 2% of their girth in five years. 2% of the height of the walls would equal just under two inches, and the design included long rods with nuts on the end inserted vertically in the walls, which would be tightened down every six months to ensure gaps did not appear in the walls. So far, so good. However, this also meant that internal walls could not go right up to the ceiling, and studwork fastened to the outside walls had to be able to slide as the walls shrank! We had to build in a two-inch gap in all internal walls, making construction more complicated and therefore more time-consuming. Secondly, Michael Phillips had designed angled walls in the shower and loo in order to provide a cupboard for the hot water tank, leading to a five-sided construction which became known as the TARDIS. In later cabins we reduced the complication by cutting out one of the diagonals, but a lot of fun was had by all in building a TARDIS which stood straight, and then later in cladding it with the pine wall boarding! To all of these challenges the happy team of volunteers rose with good humour, although by the end of a day all were pretty exhausted!

Our chosen local plumbers and electrician were a wonderful support, always turning up when they had promised, working around various volunteers in the cabins, and amusing us

A stalwart plumber

constantly with their good-natured banter – and, what's more, coming in with a bill usefully lower than their first estimate!

It was at this point that the gang from Pip n Jay's sprang into action, arriving one Saturday under the leadership of their PCC treasurer, Bruce. They built a roadway across the field from the car park to the foundations of Cabin 3 in an attempt to rescue the field from becoming a complete quagmire. Under Gerry's guidance, chippings were laid on a bed of fibreglass matting, which enabled the path to be rolled up later, and the chippings wheelbarrowed to create a path between the cabins. At least, that was the theory – the huge JCB four-wheel-drive all-wheel-steer forklift used by the Canadians still sank deeply into the roadway – but if it had not been there, I dread to think what state the field would have been in by the end!

On the 23rd of February, Cabins 1 and 2 are well ahead and we await the arrival of container three with bated breath. It's here at last – but when unpacked is found to contain the walls for the four remaining cabins only: no roofs! What's more, foreman Charles tells us he's off back to Canada on leave, having been here for four weeks, and there's no obvious replacement. The manager, Terry, with whom we had struck up a good working relationship, has also just left the supplying company for another job. The chaps on site are now leaderless, and number only four, when we were promised seven! They plod on, building increasingly muddy walls and getting slower day by day as the lack of leadership starts to show, until on 27th February two inches of snow fall in the Quantocks, whereupon the Canadians immediately leave the site because they do not have snow tyres! Five weeks left, and only two cabins available to us!

Frantic phone calls now to the suppliers' UK branch, who tell us of bad weather in Canada causing power cuts and production delays.

It wasn't until 8th March, with just four weeks to go, that the container with the roofs arrived. I suppose we thought that they

Another container arrives

would now be able to let us have Cabin 3 pretty soon – but slowness seemed the order of the day. I was calculating the number of man days needed to complete the interior of a cabin – around twenty – and seeing if we could get enough volunteers to enable something to be done, whilst at the same time believing with all my heart that the Lord wanted Storm to happen, and resisting all talk of cancelling it. We had at this stage agreed with the LEA that they would not come on site until the end of April, and that they would only have the full six cabins by mid-May.

By this time Cabins 1 and 2 were taking shape nicely, and showing us just what a superb product we were going to get. But we *did* need the next cabin to be getting on with! The suppliers still had just four men on site, despite consistent promises of more – we could cope with bad news, but it is so much harder to plan when people fob you off with promises they know they cannot fulfil. At one point we were promised men who, we found out, had just left for two weeks' holiday in Majorca!

It was on 18th March, with two weeks to go, that the two remaining Canadians told us at breakfast time that they were off back to Canada that night, leaving just two Cornish lads on site. I pleaded with them to get the windows finished in Cabin 3, and the roof beams on Cabin 4, so that, when they left, we would have a cabin to work on and the Cornish lads could get on roofing Cabin 4. They did their best, concentrating on the tricky job of cutting holes for the windows with a chainsaw – real artistry, and amazing accuracy!

Meanwhile, the Cornish lads were in the forklift, trying to get the first roof beam lined up for Cabin 4. To do this, they had to approach the side of the cabin exactly, so that the beam, which weighed half a ton, could click down neatly into the slots made for it in the gable ends. The mud between the cabins was very deep, and they ended up getting the forklift axle deeply stuck, sideways on to the cabin. The only way they could extricate it was by building scaffold towers each end of the beam and taking the weight off the forklift, by which means they managed to get the machine unbogged in time to go home – leaving the roof beam at right angles to its true position. After muttering something about having to hire a crane, they left.

That evening, I was seriously depressed. Andy and I were alone on site, and I rang home, dumping my woes on a long-suffering wife. Perhaps we were mistaken in our belief that the Lord wanted Storm to happen?

I went to bed early, and listened to the rain on the roof. By morning, the dog bowl was half-full where it had been left outside. I wandered over to the warmth of the mess hut, and sat down to have my quiet time with the Lord, gazing across the field at the rain, and at the roof beam sitting on its scaffold across the wall of Cabin 4 – the cabin we would need if we were to accommodate all the youngsters at Storm!

I was a few days behind in my *Encounter with God* readings. The reading I had got to was Luke 17 – and when I got to verse 6, the words stood out from the page: 'If you have faith as small as a mustard seed, you can say to this mulberry tree "be uprooted and planted in the sea" and it will obey you.' Well, it was pine, not mulberry – but it became plain to me that it was nothing for God to deal with moving that beam into place! We discussed it over breakfast, and resolved that we would pray specifically for the beam to be in place today.

Nine o'clock – no men. Ten o'clock came and went, as did our coffee break at eleven. It was around half past that two bleary-eyed Cornishmen turned up, having clearly hit the town the previous evening, and with serious hangovers. Somehow, the effect on them was to make them gung-ho, and they said, 'Better give it another go.' Despite the deeper and wetter mud, and the quagmire they had created the previous day, they drove the forklift into position, picked up the beam, and slotted it right into place – just like that! By lunchtime it was secure, and we were praising the Lord – and asking Him for the second one, which would fit at right angles to

A giant jigsaw

108

the first. But the Cornishmen told us that health and safety provisions would not allow them to do the second one, because it would have to be bolted to the first at high level, even if they were able to get it into position.

We prayed on, and mid-afternoon, quite unannounced and unexpected, Charles the Canadian foreman arrived, having just landed back from Canada, and having decided to call in at Great Wood on his way to the office to see how things were progressing. When he saw how little they had achieved whilst he had been away, he took the two lads into the middle of the field and we could feel the dressing-down from the other side! Once he had finished, they crept back into the cab of the forklift, and by close of play they had the second roof beam in place. What prompted Charles to call in? I think I know – thanks be to God.

It was at the beginning of the following week that the Lord spoke to us again from the *Encounter* readings. In chapter 18 of Luke's gospel he records the encounter Jesus has with the blind beggar, when Jesus asks him a rather strange question: 'What do you want me to do for you?' I think for the first time I fully realised the intimacy of specific direct requests to the Lord for the resolution of simple daily problems – without the usual get-out clauses such as 'if it be Thy will'. So we started the practice of discussing over breakfast what three things we needed that day to be able to keep the momentum up, and asking the Lord specifically that he would answer them today. Only three things? This enabled us to look for and appreciate the answers, rather than making any assessment as to the capacity of the Lord to deliver! It was quite humbling and amazing the answers we got – in fact, I do not think anything went unresolved except for the problem with the flooring, of which more later.

As an example, I have already explained the difficulty caused by the shrinkage of the outer shell of the cabins. The suppliers fixed the outside doors, but we had to deal with the fitting of two interior doors within the log frame, where the hall is divided from the bunkrooms. It was clear that fitting these doors was beyond the expertise of any of us. This became the subject of one of our specific prayer requests: 'Please, Lord, enable us to fix the problem!'

During coffee that morning, Gerry looked out of the window and saw someone wandering across the field, and went out to ask whether he could help.

'I've just moved into the area, and am curious to see these cabins. I'm a carpenter, and used to work for Norwegian Log,' the man replied.

'Can you hang doors?' Gerry asked.

'Yes, I'm looking for work opportunities in the area!'

Problem solved – Paul joined the team and did a brilliant job.

Some other remarkable examples:

- The field was in a terrible state towards the end of the build programme. In praying about it we were sent an amazingly skilful JCB driver, Simon, who did wonders in sorting it out, digging paths and moving materials. When Ray Haines turned

The quagmire

up on site and saw the situation, he was naturally concerned about the schools coming, and the access to the cabins. Again a specific request for an acceptable solution. In discussing options, he suggested we make a gravel path between the cabins – a solution that not only was possible to construct in a relatively short time, but also looked good.

- We often calculated the number of volunteers we needed at any one time, in order to maximise output without hopeless congestion in the cabins. We'd ask the Lord to send us folk, some of whom merely turned up having been 'talking to Caroline; can I help?' Colin, Ian, Stuart, Peter and Rosie joined us, to say nothing of stray Great Wood folk who came in for a day or an evening, such as Pete Barker. Pete came with a mini digger (much to Charlie's delight!) and some excellent power tools, which he left with us for some time.

There were also frequent requests for the safe delivery of much-needed materials – missing parts for the bunks, curtains which had been sent away for fireproofing, lockers – to say nothing of the laying of turf in time for the grand opening on 8th May, which looked pretty impossible due to the appalling weather and the deep mud, but which was achieved in pouring rain by a gang who decided to pull out the stops for us.

Safety was another minor miracle. With so many volunteers using some pretty sophisticated power tools, overcrowded cabins, and electricians up ladders dodging enthusiastic DIY carpenters with four-metre lengths of wood, it was amazing that no one got more than a hammer dropped on them!

It was not until 24th March – with just eight days to go before Storm's arrival – that Cabin 4 was finally handed over to us. We agreed with Storm that they would be able to cope without plumbing or full electrics, as they had for many years in the old cabins! As it turned out, our electrician, Derek, was able to provide basic lighting. We hit it with all the energy we could muster – a day

Setting the trustees to work

to lay the under flooring, joists, Kingspan, under-floor electrics, a day and a half for flooring, after which the ceiling was made up, stud walls added, and the long business of cladding started. With another day needed for sanding and finishing the floor, and a day for furnishings and curtains, I still do not know how we made it – perhaps the sun stood still? Jan and I were just removing our tools on the 2nd of April when we saw the first campers coming across the field with their rucksacks on their backs! Talk about Ground Force!

Meanwhile, over the weekend of 26th to 28th March, a mini work party led by Mike Menzies had hit the task of building the patios, first digging out around the cabins to make a level area and then building the paving that we had selected from Travis Perkins. We used surplus timber to form the edges to a perimeter path, and created a path with chippings we salvaged from the temporary road which had been built across the field. We owe a debt of gratitude here to Pip n Jay's church in Bristol, who sent a work party one Saturday to wheelbarrow huge quantities of gravel and to lift the fibreglass matting which had been used as a base for this road, now embedded in the mud!

Joel Carter remembers arriving as a camper to something that resembled a battlefield, with trenches and debris scattered around. 'The path to our cabin was an obstacle course made up of pallets and planks; you had to pick your way over the quagmire beneath. As we were in Cabin 4 (Cabin 5 was just a shell and 6 was little more than a concrete plinth at this point) we had no running water. This was nothing of concern, having been well acquainted with the previous cabins. What caused more of a potential hindrance to the enjoyment of the week was the beds that at this point still lay flat packed in their boxes. Challenge one of the week: "make your bed". Thankfully I passed.'

After Storm, we returned to finish off the remaining cabins, and by early May we were able to hand over the completed units to the LEA for the school season.

And so to the thanksgiving day! The field no longer looked like a First World War battlefield. In discussion with Keith Civval, we had decided to spend extra money on turfing, which we were able to achieve just in time before the opening ceremony. About 200 people crowded onto the site on a bitterly cold May day, to give thanks to the Lord for all He had provided. The rain held off, which was a great blessing, and everyone there rose to the pioneering spirit of the occasion.

Various snagging problems remained, the worst of which was mould, which appeared in various places towards the end of the 2004 season. We spent considerable time assessing the reasons for this, and drew up plans for the introduction of ventilators under the eaves of the sleeping areas. As it turned out, the problem was short-lived, and did not recur in subsequent years. It had apparently been caused by the cabins not having had sufficient time to dry out!

Treating the new cabins

Outside timber treatment followed over a weekend in 2004; this now forms part of the Easter work party's regular maintenance work. We had to strip and retreat one of the floors over winter 2004/05, anti-mice sealant had to be applied to the pipe outlet areas, and some remedial work to the roofs still remains, but on the whole the new cabins have worked well and have substantially expanded the flexibility of Great Wood to accept groups of varying types and backgrounds. Looking at the number and variety of holidays now being run compared with in 2000 is exciting!

What Next?

Having completed the cabins, the planning group turned its attention to the other side of the field. We asked Michael Phillips to sit outside one of the cabins and criticise the visual appearance of the mess hut side. He advised (from top of the field to the bottom):

- The new bosun's store is an eyesore,
- Remove the old caravan,
- The JI hut needs a makeover from the outside, not just remodelling inside,
- Do not connect the JI hut to the mess hut,
- The tractor shed should go, and
- The rubbish shed is an eyesore.

We asked Michael to do a design for the remodelling of the JI hut, which resulted in a change in the fenestration and the addition of a porch. We commissioned this work from Gilbert over the winter of 2004/05. The grotty sleeping quarters were stripped out, the building remodelled, insulated and clad with surplus pine cladding from the cabin building programme. We had retained and stored all surplus materials in a cheap marquee on site, and we had just finished sorting these when a snowfall caused the collapse of the marquee!

Whereas the cost of the work on the JI hut was some £10,000 more than our original plans, the result was way beyond our expectations. We now have a comfortable meeting area, decent storage and a main building which feels good, with access which enables folk to leave mud and rain behind before they enter! We also have a giant chessboard outside!

We were persuaded to remove the caravan – much to the dismay of some of Storm's newly married team! It housed the only double bed on site!

We then spent considerable time and energy in discussing the tractor shed, the bosun's store and the workshop. We wanted to create a disabled toilet in the workshop, as it was part of the existing toilet block and easily accessible for a wheelchair user. Where to store the stuff? And how could we justify the removal of a perfectly sound building just because it was ugly? In the end, we opted for a remodelling of the interior of the remaining part of the workshop and the bosun's store to increase their effectiveness, and left the tractor shed alone. Doing this meant creating storage for blankets and pillows within the new cabins, which was where they should have been stored anyway. This work was carried out entirely by the volunteer team. The rubbish shed was remodelled as part of the recycling arrangements we put in place in co-operation with Kilve from spring 2007.

In 2007 advice was taken from swimming pool specialists. We opted for a system with the following characteristics:

- Automatic chemical dosing.
- Low-energy heating – we were installing a heat pump.
- High security. We did not want to rely on a high fence, as this would obscure visual supervision from elsewhere on site, so the contractors advised a roll-over cover which would provide security and heat retention.
- Observation area, using the bank of spoil deposited when the cabins were built.
- Separate pump house, to minimise noise.

Joel Carter noted that there was no doubt about it; the upgrade of the pool with a heating (honest) system was a positive development. However, it didn't change the use of the pool as a bath. This was a feature that, after the chaotic mayhem of the mud fights that occurred at Youth Focus and Storm, was put to full advantage. The result would be a pool so full of mud that the quickest way to clean it was to empty it and shovel out the mud, which would be up to two inches deep in places. Thankfully, with the pool being fed directly from the stream, we didn't have to pay to refill it.

In 2007 there was also detailed work on sewage disposal systems and consideration was given to various solutions, from

The new pool

reed beds to new septic tanks, but it was concluded that the best long-term solution would be a bio-digester, which was installed.

A New Vision

'Tom Thayer took over from Caroline, built on her work and also found himself drawn into development and maintenance of the site,' Lesley Blight writes. 'A vision day held at Great Wood in November 2005 also produced several proposals for ministry development, which, while in line with the rest of Scripture Union's strategic objectives, were likely to involve additional financial risk and the appointment of additional field staff. Scripture Union's board had to weigh up these desired developments in the light of needs and aspirations elsewhere in the movement and ensure an overall balance of its ministries.

117

'With volunteers already playing such a key role in managing activity at Great Wood (in the form of GWEG, the Great Wood Estate Group), it was in some ways an obvious step from there to the idea of Great Wood becoming a kind of specialist associate ministry and more independent. An obvious step, maybe, but by no means a small one. Some members of GWEG took the bold decision to become the first trustees of a newly formed Great Wood charitable trust. The Great Wood Trust formally came into being in July 2007.

'A licence agreement was drawn up whereby Scripture Union continued to own the site while the Great Wood Trust took responsibility for overseeing ministry development. Scripture Union would continue to use the site for its holidays programme, and so – making use of the flexibility and opportunity that other places did not offer – new events began. A series of family Bible holidays got underway and "Wide Open" was established, a very special new annual holiday for young people with learning difficulties (of which more later).

'The licence agreement was for an initial three years and was then renewed … before the next change came along for the Great Wood Trust.'

The Mess Hut

One of the problems we encounter when we replace some buildings with smart new ones is that the older ones show their age. The new cabins had a meaningful impact on the way campers behaved, as they had become more appealing as living space than the mess hut, which by that stage was nearly fifty years old. We decided action was needed. A working group was appointed, led by Jon Chambers, to examine the options.

In January 2008 the working group sent out a questionnaire to camp leaders, and reported to the Trust shortly after that. In their report they stipulated the following remit for the project:

1. Any building on the site must remain part of an overall visual image in keeping with the setting and environment. Visual impact is a key issue for planning.
2. It is to be assumed that the existing building will remain, with any alterations being carried out without major demolition.
3. This brief is limited to consideration of the main meeting area of the existing mess hut, together with the drying room, boot porch and shop behind, and extending to the patio area outside to the west and south.
4. The redeveloped mess hut needs to regain its function as a focal point of the community. It also needs to include an obvious entrance for visitors (to avoid traffic through the kitchen).
5. The current use of the kitchen as an access point to the mess hut building needs to be stopped. Improved alternative access routes are envisaged.
6. This development is to have an effective working life of at least fifty years (in other words, a short-term fix is not envisaged). If the budget is deemed insufficient we would prefer to delay the project rather than compromise the specifications.

Their timeframe envisaged a start in October 2009 with completion by March 2010. The budget was £80,000, which was the amount the Trust had in hand at that time.

When the first architect was consulted, he quickly pointed out that the existing building had a very light frame, consisting of four-by-two timber clad with a very lightweight material. Furthermore, he advised that, if any alterations required building regulations approval, the whole building, including the kitchen, would need to comply. It was a non-starter.

Jon and his team went back to the drawing board, convinced that now we had to dream of a whole new building.

They presented an architect's brief for a completely new building in June 2009, with a revised budget of £500,000. Gulp! This time their timetable envisaged a start in September 2011, with our having raised the funds in the meantime. Mike Hope of Roderick James Architects was appointed in 2009, and the story continues ...

Vision and Strategy for the Great Wood Trust

We were determined not to lose sight of our key focus whilst all the discussions regarding the mess hut were going on. By the end of 2009 we had defined our vision and strategy as follows:

The Vision

The vision of the Trust is to create and maintain a pathway by which people of all ages may move from total ignorance of the Gospel of Jesus to mature discipleship, and which they can join and leave at any time.

The Strategy

Although the Great Wood Trust is an independently managed charitable trust company, it has agreed with Scripture Union to work closely in a ministry partnership in order to achieve its vision. SU has licensed the Trust to occupy Great Wood Camp during the majority of each year, excluding only those parts of school holidays when SU themselves wish to run holidays there. This working partnership is a foundational aspect of the strategy for the Trust.

Increasing Diversity

Redthread

The increased flexibility at camp led to some new opportunities. Redthread is a Christian youth project in south London and has run its camp (for pupils from Year 7 to Year 9) at Great Wood since

2004. Mary Rennison, a leader, wrote, 'I ran a Friday night youth group in Dulwich, south-east London, which was linked to St Barnabas church. We also ran an after-school café. Some of the work I did was with churched youth, and those people I invited to Storm and Space, but the unchurched young people I wanted to take on residentials. Great Wood is a long way from south-east London (and I did use other venues/adventure centres), but I really wanted to share Great Wood with these unchurched young people because it is an amazing site in an amazing location, because I was offered amazing rates that made it financially doable, because I felt there was something spiritual about the site ... kind of soaked in the Holy Spirit and the prayers of the saints over the years, and because then it would be easy to invite young people to Storm and Space if they had already been there.

'We have to limit camper places to thirty-six just to keep to coach limitations and a suitable adult-to-child ratio. It is unfortunate, although also encouraging, that we regularly have to turn down a number of young people.

'For young people from London, or any urban area, from deprived or privileged family backgrounds, the Great Wood experience is a truly great one, where the views, stars, trees and quiet have an awesome influence in deepening young people's thoughts to the bigger questions of life, creation etc. A number of the senior team are familiar with the site, but it is amazing to see how much the team of youth workers, all with considerable camp experience elsewhere, have come to appreciate and love the site and see it as the best option for our young people to return to, each year, for camp.

'The camps were all run along these lines. We are unashamedly a Christian organisation. All the leaders are Christian and we pray together each day for you and for the camp. You are here to have fun and enjoy yourself, and hopefully you will see God in the setting and the people. At some point (and maybe several times) in any weekend or week we will challenge you to think about the really deep questions of life, really to ask questions. We hope that might lead you to return to an SU Christian camp here, to talk and ask questions of the leaders, or to come along to Christian events back in Dulwich.

'I relied very heavily on friends from Storm and Space coming as leaders on camp. I followed the examples of leadership of camps that I had learnt from John and Jan Simmons (Storm) and also Sue and Andy Keighley (Space), about there being no "them" and "us", about leaders eating, sitting, chatting and walking alongside young people, about great hospitality, about going above and beyond in terms of food, set-up, décor to make people feel special.

'The young people we brought to camp were from a wide variety of backgrounds, from the exclusive private schools of Dulwich to the local estates. Some had special needs, at times it was chaotic and crazy, *but* lots of young people came and had a great holiday. Lots went on to do Storm and Space. Lots became Christians. It was exciting. Great Wood offered the Redthread team a place that enabled that transition from non-Christian work to giving people the option to go deeper and find a relationship with God.

'My best story is of a young person who came on camp from a family who were quite anti-church. I had long chats with his mum about whether he should come. On the first night we were very late arriving at camp but decided to go ahead with a night wide game we'd planned. It was midnight and this boy walked into a tree and split his head open. There was blood everywhere. It was really horrific. Chris Owen jumped into action and the boy was driven to hospital in Taunton. I had to call his mum and dad at one or two in the morning to explain what had happened. They were so gracious to me. He has a *Harry Potter*-style scar on his forehead now. But because he missed all of the camp, he insisted that he come on Storm at Easter, which his parents would never have allowed otherwise. He became a Christian there at some point over the next few years. He was baptised and confirmed at St Barnabas and his maternal granddad played a part in the services because he was a vicar. The boy's mum had been anti-God because of her dad's job, but after that regularly came to church. God clearly had a plan for her life as well. I am not sure whether that fantastic young man still has a faith. I think of him often.'

Joel Carter also recalls an incident at a Redthread camp. 'It was given to me to lead a walk: a stealth walk, to be precise. A stealth walk has very little to do with stealth and everything to do with not using the paths. As we set off with most of the camp in tow I had a hunch that some of them didn't know what they were letting themselves in for. As the girls set off, their faces pristinely presented, there were a few murmurings asking where on earth we were going. Before long the group were thoroughly disoriented and had no choice but to follow me. As we continued, the wet leaves from the rhododendron and the muddy ground worked their magic and broke down the barriers of trying to be cool, and they all started to have fun. I knew the job was done when we reached some long, deep puddles that had been carved into the path by some forestry machinery. One by one I watched everyone jump flat out into the puddles, makeup pouring down their faces and smiles all round.'

Refugee Holidays

'For a couple of years in 2006 and 2007 a Bournemouth-based group, helping refugees to integrate into English society, stayed for a long weekend at the end of the summer,' Joel Carter writes. 'Very different from many of the other camps and groups that use the site, the team worked with a multi-faith group of refugees from all over the world. Some refugees had been living in the country for thirteen years and others had been in the country for less than a week. With such a variety of guests from such varied backgrounds we had a few challenges with communication; not everyone spoke the same verbal language. That being said, these visits hold for me some great memories and by far the best barbecues I have ever had.

'Looking at stories from the Bible that focused on characters that are key players in other religions allowed us to open discussions about our faith in a way that was respectful to all. Learning why some of the guests believed what they did has been of great benefit to my personal faith and helped in my approach to others who don't share my faith in Jesus.

'Culturally it was a very interesting, if tiring, mix. I remember getting up for team meetings at 7.30, later than some camps, and running through the normal day of planned activities, which can be tiring enough as it is. However, because there was no requirement to join in anything other than the main evening meetings, some of the guests didn't get up until 11am and as a result were happy to stay up much later. Every night a fire would be lit, food produced, drinks drunk and the inevitable rhythms tapped out on whatever was closest, leading to plenty of dancing from every corner of the globe. Evenings like this, filled with great conversation and opportunities for sharing our lives, are not something you want to pass up. So it would often be the not-so-early hours of the morning before I got to bed, heavy-eyed and dreading the thought of getting up in four or five hours' time. That said, if they ever chose to return to Great Wood, I would happily sacrifice a few hours' sleep to enjoy the conversations and fellowship again.'

Thoughts on Utilising Great Wood for the Disabled

It came to the attention of the Great Wood Estate Group that some physically disabled children were attending the camp as part of the schools programme. The Local Education Authority asked for better provision. So the chapel cabin was adapted in 2002 with a single-bedded room, a converted shower room and toilet, and an access ramp.

Jan Simmons recalls how Scripture Union, under the insightful guidance of Lesley Blight as Head of Missions and Holidays, appointed a person to lead a ministry to those with disabilities. 'Denise Abrahall had worked as a special school teacher and was keen to provide a holiday for those who were unable to access the usual SU holidays because of an additional need that could not be addressed without specialist resources. She approached me and proposed using Great Wood. I had experience of working in a special school as a speech and language therapist and had been looking for an opportunity to use the things I had learnt in a Christian context. However, I was startled by her idea of using Great Wood, as all I could see were the obvious dangers of an insecure site with a swimming pool and a stream, bunk beds and a bumpy field. Patiently she sat me down and we discussed the issues. Having looked at a school site, Denise felt that a complicated layout of corridors, staircases, enormous grounds and many rooms was a real problem for those with a learning disability and would mean a young person would need to be accompanied at all times just to find their way around, whereas at camp the young people were either in their cabins, doing activities on the field, or in the mess hut or JI hut. All are in line of sight.

'Our first Wide Open Holiday was held in August 2005 and we had fourteen young campers and a team of people, some with experience but others with little or none at all. Our main aim was to run a holiday that was tailored to be as accessible as possible, with multi-sensory teaching, signs and symbols, strict programming and carefully planned activities that would encourage a sense of adventure and independence for our young people.

'In the past thirteen years we have striven to improve and have adjusted our methods and programme. We have found that as our reputation has spread we are working with a greater range of disability and more challenging medical and behavioural conditions. By the grace of God we are able to show Christ's love for these youngsters. We present the gospel to them in as clear a way as we can, but time and time again we are overwhelmed by the knowledge that God reveals himself directly to them in ways we cannot understand. Many of the youngsters have very limited verbal understanding, some have very little speech and others rely on signing, but witnessing our Flag Worship session and our singing worship leads us to conclude that the Holy Spirit is enabling them to respond to Him.

'During Wide Open we use the swimming pool a great deal. The safety cover and the single depth are valuable to us. We use the archery, the low ropes and the nightline (although during the day). For the first few years the zipwire was very popular, and we missed it when it was pronounced a health and safety risk. We have a camp fire, walk and picnic in the forest and make our own lunch.'

Wide Open walk

Over the years Joel Carter has been lucky enough to go to many a camp, but he takes great delight when God surprises him with something new. He writes, 'Helping at Wide Open I noticed two of the more mischievous campers wander off into the chapel. Thinking it best that this was not left unchecked for too long, I wandered over to join them. What met me there wasn't any sort of mischievous behaviour or even a rehearsal for a Chuckle Brothers sketch for the last night but a quiet service in which they took it in turns to pray and read the scriptures. When they saw me they did what we should all do in such settings and invited me to join them, giving me a chance to pray and say thank you to God.'

'For many years, Paula Smith was a part of the core leadership group,' Jan Simmons adds. 'She was born with cerebral palsy and is a wheelchair user. She was the eyes and ears of the team and proved beyond doubt that having a multi-faceted team was a benefit. She was involved in all areas of camp life, but at huge personal cost. The energy required to propel herself around the field and paths was enormous. If anyone could cope at Great Wood in a wheelchair then it would be Paula with her gutsy determination, but it was far from easy. We have come to realise that although in our hearts we want to be able to welcome all those with any disability, it will always be extremely hard for those with severe physical difficulties.'

The Other Side to Serious

Joel Carter comments on how we have serious lives and serious jobs and we introduce ourselves as serious people, but every now and then, like when we are at Great Wood, we get the chance just to enjoy life and show everyone we are not always so serious.

'Often when the announcement that we are going for a walk is made there is grumbling from a few people, and on rare occasions this progresses to point-blank refusal to join in. This was exactly the situation at Wide Open one year, but, knowing that no one likes to feel left out, we set off leaving a member of the team behind to make sure the camper in question went the right way when they finally followed. About ten minutes after setting off, we heard over the radio that the camper had started up the hill and would be joining us in due course. Happy we were now all underway, we thought nothing more of it until over the radio came a series of monkey noises. To our great amusement the noises came both from the camper and from a certain ordained ex-accountant, John Simmons. John had a habit of being rather cheeky, especially in the evening team meetings, but thankfully his wife Jan needed do no more than glance in his direction to keep him in check – most of the time.'

An Evening's Entertainment

'Once the campers are in bed and the team have gathered and debriefed, the remainder of the evening is generally passed relaxing and getting to know each other,' Joel Carter writes. 'During this time it is commonplace for the team to enjoy "Officers' Nosh" (eat up the leftover food). Sometimes entertainment is made, but sometimes entertainment provides itself.

'On one particular evening at Wide Open one of the campers had decided he didn't want to go to bed just yet, and when Bruce said no he meant *no*. One of our team, Simon Wells, decided he would try and give him a little encouragement, so he warned Bruce of the wolves that live in the hills and come down when all the lights are turned off. Simon then proceeded to walk around the site, turning off each light in turn, while Bruce sat on the bench between the mess hut and the JI hut. When all the lights were off Simon stood behind a cabin and began to howl ... and Bruce continued to sit on the bench.

'Resigning himself to the fact that Bruce was determined to stick it out, Simon returned to the kitchen to join the team meeting. We were at the time hosting a member of the SU holiday team who had come to stay for the night. A short while later Bruce walked in and stood in the doorway. Holding his hands to his head as ears, he exclaimed, "There was a wolf … and he had big ears," then, bringing his hands down, he continued, "and big claws … and it was him!" He pointed across the room to Simon. With this the entire team fell apart with laughter while Bruce calmly stepped over the bench and, taking a plate, helped himself to some food. Sitting down, he looked around with an expression of "so, what are we talking about?" Not having any other real option, we gathered ourselves and continued. A little later, while we were praying, Bruce obviously decided he had eaten enough and took himself off to bed. Clearly he wasn't scared of meeting any wolves.

'Some years later, while we were having a similar team meeting, again whilst hosting a member of the SU holiday team, a flicker of colour flashed past the door to the back passage. Moments later there it was again, but this time it was clearly the figure of a camper dressed in all the splendour of his outfit intended for the last night. As he marched up and down the back passage in his Joseph robes he was sweeping the floor with a brush he had found. When James approached him to ask what he was doing, the camper simply instructed him as a king would a servant.'

An Unusual Answer to Prayer

In the early 2000s GWX, formerly the Backwoodsman camp, lasted ten days and included a football tournament. Anthony Greenhill's cabin of younger boys remarkably made it to the final, which had to be decided with a penalty shootout. 'This went on until the potentially deciding shot had to be kicked by the cabin member least able to do it,' Anthony recalls. 'His shot somehow trickled past the goalie into the goal, and we won the tournament! "Yes! God is real!" shouted one boy. He had been praying we would win!'

Harmless Fun

'As has been the tradition for many years, the younger, more energetic members of the team have a tendency to stay up late and plot mischief,' Joel Carter writes. 'However, as the night draws on there is often a tendency to be a little more fanciful with ideas, such as cutting every shoe on site in half and stitching them back together in odd pairs. Some ideas were a little more successful, like the child-sized mannequin dressed each day in lost property and transported around the site, from the zipwire to the flag pole to the mess hut roof, and even up a tree during one of the wide games.

'On one particular occasion we decided to get out all the old foot and mouth signs, placing them around site with buckets of "disinfectant" (food colouring and water), and with a few handfuls of hay from the local farmer we set about making stations at each entrance to the mess hut. The following morning was spent watching bleary-eyed team members and campers alike walk up to the signs and pause, normally with a confused look on their face, before shuffling slowly through the straw as they entered for breakfast. What met them inside was a wall of spectators looking out the window at the next unwitting participant and a wave of realisation that in their sleep-deprived state they may have been duped. It wasn't, however, until we returned to our regular lives that we realised that the most unlikely of events had occurred. For while we were setting up our signs, on the other side of the country, a genuine outbreak of foot and mouth had just been discovered.'

Some Things Don't Change

Joel Carter returned from spending a summer at camp and told how he went to see his grandmother, Mary Gibson. 'When I was regaling her with my adventures I shared a story from The Real Thing, a summer camp for thirteen-to-fifteen-year-olds. Whilst laying the tables for breakfast the team had carefully included one of the team members on the table, complete with sleeping bag and pillow. To my great amusement Grandma then proceeded to share the same story from when she was helping on team. It would appear we were not the first and probably won't be the last to try that one.

'So often it is the case that the things that happen at camp appear rather strange when you get home and reintegrate into society. For a few years it was very common for people to arrive home to find pegs attached to their clothes, and on one occasion someone arrived home to find that a peg attached to their rear windscreen wiper had managed to remain in place even with the wipers being used.'

Long associations with camp are common, and the newsletters mentioned in appendix 1 aid that involvement in the Great Wood family even when one is unable to attend. Anthony Greenhill first went to Great Wood as a 'junior officer' (aged eighteen) to the 'A' camp led by JI for prep school boys aged eleven to thirteen. 'At that time we lived in Nether Stowey but attended Over Stowey church, where JI was rector. I went several times each year up to 1963, then had a long break, apart from two camps when on "furlough" from India. I started going again every year after retiring in 2001.'

Confusing the Locals

Initiatives in the hills have been a staple of GWX for as long as Joel can remember, wandering the hills attempting to find checkpoints where your mental and physical aptitude will be tested. 'On some occasions the first challenge is to find the member of team who, despite informing everyone they could map read, ended up a good mile and a half from the grid reference they were given.

'In recent years at GWX Tom Harrison and Jack Phillips, along with a variety of willing volunteers, have developed this wonderful activity into increasingly elaborate adventures. Themes have ranged greatly but have often left the locals a little bemused.

131

On one occasion, whilst waiting for the next cabin to find me, I was met by two forestry workers. After a cursory look at my attire they greeted me with, "You must be with the two Jedi down the hill, but what *are* you doing?" Even after my brief explanation I think they probably thought it more likely we had escaped from the local psychiatric ward.'

The Lord of the Rim

'One of the great opportunities The Real Thing offers is a two-day expedition across Exmoor and, in recent years, the Quantocks,' Joel writes. 'But simply walking across moorland can become monotonous for some, and attempts to liven it up have no doubt baffled and amused many who have encountered cabin groups on their way to Lynmouth. Chris Owen led a cabin across Exmoor carrying an old chair with a hole cut in the seat to be used for practical purposes, each member playing their part as they recreated "The Lord of the Rim". Others have taken bouncy hoppers, unicycles and walking planks. Perhaps more foolishly, others have forgone what might seem like basic equipment and attempted the expedition without shoes or sleeping bags.

'One of the great benefits of the walk is time really getting to know your cabin group and bonding over the shared experience. Every cabin will have a slightly different route and a very different experience, which can lead to a variety of expectations. One particular year a number from the oldest girls' cabin decided they should carry with them a change of clothes and their makeup so that when they stopped at Watersmeet they could make themselves a little more presentable for when they finally arrived at Lynmouth, or more specifically for when they met the boys from the oldest cabin. What they didn't count on was the result of the boys' cabin having had a fire the night before and consequently having spent the evening collecting wood in the dark. One particular member had found an old fence post in the field and picked it up not noticing where it had been lying, or more specifically what it had been lying in. The result was that the girls were met not by their dashing counterparts but by a T-shirt covered in day-old cow manure.'

When You Can't Remember the Names

Joel has never been very good at remembering names, let alone when you have to try to learn at least eight new names every week. 'One solution for this arose at The Real Thing when I was leading a cabin with my brother. With the theme of the week being cowboys and Indians, we decided it was only natural to rename each of the campers as they arrived with an Indian name. We were "Big Chief Rising Sun" and "Big Chief Waxing Moon" and the campers each had their own little chief name: "Rattle Snake", "Bear Cub", "Wolf Cub", "Eagle Scout" etc. Whilst the names brought about much hilarity in the week they continued to stick with the boys (loosely) for many years as they came back as senior campers and team.'

Working with Wood

'The Great Wood family is always looking to help others even though they may never meet,' Joel writes. 'This spirit spreads throughout all the camps, every camp doing their best to clean the site as well as they can regardless of how they think the site was left for them (always amusing how people see the dirt and not everything that's clean around it). After a particularly heavy snowfall one winter there were a number of trees that had either fallen or been cut down. Seeing an opportunity at GWX, we gathered fourteen of the more able-bodied team and dragged out one of the trees from the swamp area to replace an aging fire surround. The number of breaks we needed to get it across the field, despite having a very fit and strong team, highlighted the immensity of the environment in which we live.'

Joel was asked to help design and build a small treehouse as an activity for Space, a task in which he was thoroughly excited to take part. 'By the end of the week we had created little more than a platform with a rope ladder to access it. With the absence of any sort of sides it was fairly limited in its potential. That being said, it remained in place for a couple of years and was a wonderful place for a quiet afternoon nap after a pub lunch. Several years later it was decided to make something more of it and the work party set about adding walls and a lockable ladder. It now provides a wonderful place to look out over the field or have a small group in a truly unique place. Certainly much more than we had expected when we set about attaching the first trusses. In much the same

The treehouse takes shape

way there are countless campers who leave Great Wood as platforms, never to return, but God has plans to develop them into great treehouses, and it is our great joy and privilege to help them on their first steps while they are with us.

'The tradition of a camp fire on the last night has been around as long as camps at Great Wood, and normally campers are enlisted to help collect wood at opportune moments throughout the week. On one occasion we sat looking at the rather pathetic pile of wood collected due largely to a limited amount of time available. With a very busy programme as we always had, we had only the time after the evening team meeting to collect some more of the larger logs needed. So head torches went on and a handful of enthusiastic if not very refreshed volunteers set out to collect the final bits needed. Thanks largely to God's protection we came back safely a couple of hours later with enough wood to build the fire and in need of some refreshment.

'At the beginning of every week teams spend some time getting the site ready for their programme. Occasionally, if there is a little time to kill, solutions become a little over-engineered! A great example was when GWX needed to wash the tea towels but, given the excellent weather, didn't want to use the tumble dryer. So the task was set to the senior campers to extend the washing line: a simple enough task, putting a stake in the ground and connecting the line. They, however, decided it would be a great chance to demonstrate their knots prowess. An hour or so later a fourteen-foot tripod had been erected and tested by members of the team jumping on and swinging off. Clearly years of doing their knots test had paid off.'

The Damming of the Stream

For as long as there has been a camp at Great Wood, the stream has been dammed. 'It's not everyone's cup of tea and some dams have been little more than a line of stones across the stream,' Joel writes, 'but some have decided that they want to make a statement with their dam. This may mean getting the water deep enough to go over the top of your wellies, or creating another dam further upstream, or breaking the banks, but some go one step further. With key positioning and a lot of dam building, Cabin 5 managed to create a reservoir deep and vast enough actually to swim in. The result of the dam building and nature's own course has led to an ever-changing stream which has been capitalised on by the introduction of the nightline really allowing people to experience a side of nature they wouldn't normally.

'On one occasion it wasn't the water in the stream that was causing the issues on site. One year it rained so hard that it began to put the cabins at risk of flooding. Thankfully Reuben and Jack were unafraid of getting a bit wet, and a series of trenches were dug to divert the flow of water around the cabins and on to the stream.'

At one Backwoodsman camp a few years before Cabin 5's achievement, Elizabeth Carter remembers, the local fire brigade had volunteered to come and give the boys a talk about fire safety in the forest. 'They dammed up the stream with a ladder and tarpaulin behind Cabin 3 to show how they created a water reservoir, and then showed the boys how to use the hoses. You guessed it: before long there was a huge water fight with the crew and a lot of laughter all round.'

Senior Campers or Junior Team

There has been a debate in recent years as to whether younger helpers are senior campers or junior team, Joel says. 'It's a moot point in all practicality, but what is certain is the purpose of developing team from a young age. In line with Commy's original vision, discipling and training team from an early age is key to their development as Christians and their effectiveness as potential leaders in future years. However, along the way they don't always get it right.

'The old potato peeler was a wonderful machine and in the hands of experienced team could allow two people to peel and chop potatoes for eighty in half an hour or, in the case of one group of senior campers, turn a batch of large potatoes into new potatoes in twenty minutes.

'Washing up as senior campers is normally good fun because of some good music, a steady flow of leftover food and a lot of jokes along the way, together with a little light-hearted towel flicking. However, if you are of the same ilk as Ben, or Bingo, as he was always known, washing up is all about finding onto what you can stick a plunger. The result: a plunger sticking to his cheek and a grin across his face.'

2010s: Young People Come Alive

That God is certainly real at Great Wood is evident in answered prayer about the weather. '2012 produced a pretty wet summer,' recalls Anthony Greenhill, 'but I had been praying for months for *dry* weather for GWX. We had clear blue skies throughout the camp – which was far from the case elsewhere! Now I tend to pray for the *right* weather. In 2017 we had a fairly wet camp, but it *never* rained when we needed it to be dry! (Though one year it pelted down just as the final camp fire was lit (with "magic water"), and we all had to watch it from the mess hut!)

'We do some potentially dangerous things at Great Wood, but accidents are surprisingly rare. I was once taking a boy through the axemanship test. He missed the wood he was chopping and buried the axe in his ankle! I pulled up the leg of his jeans, which revealed a three-inch vertical gash just above the ankle – amazingly it wasn't bleeding. He later said it didn't hurt until he saw it! I helped him hobble to the first aid room – by which time the wound was bleeding, so of course that had to be stopped – then it was off to Taunton Hospital for stitches. There was another accident with an axe the same day, but I think these were the only ones in at least twenty-five camps I've been at over many years.'

'There are often chances for people to try new things when they go to Great Wood,' Joel Carter writes, 'and often they are a great experience that can be the start of a new hobby or interest. Thanks to the generosity of James Aston, people could have a go at fly fishing while at Space. Unfortunately for one camper, whilst he was waiting his turn, a somewhat erratic attempt by another participant resulted in a fly cast into his neck. Thankfully there were no hard feelings between him and the would-be angler.'

Anthony continues, 'Great Wood demonstrates that you can experience God in a lot of fun. On Johnny Owen's final camp we had a sort of sedan chair – a throne supported by two poles that could be carried by four people. On the last day we sat Johnny on the throne and then all the boys and leaders gleefully paraded him round the field – before tipping him into the swimming pool!'

Always Fun, Not Always to Plan

Joel Carter says he was lucky enough to have his stag do at Great Wood, a truly enjoyable weekend with some amazing guys in an amazing place. 'The plan was to try and pack a week of activities into a weekend, so obviously we ended the Saturday night with a camp fire. The issue was that the weather in October was not ideal and just when we were trying to light the fire the heavens opened, soaking us to the core. Determined to make the most of the fire we had built, we stood a couple of feet away and slowly rotated in a continuous state of both drying and soaking. It may not have been quite what was planned, but we still had fun and lots of laughs.'

Calm

'It has always been abundantly evident to me that Great Wood is a special place, an opinion that is clearly shared by many,' Joel Carter writes. 'When Storm had to finish, this fact was particularly highlighted. In the space of a month from when I had a conversation with David Casey to say we should just go and spend a week with Great Wood folk, we found ourselves with half the camp full and caterers willing to cook for us. The work party, Le Weekend and Love Great Wood are all further examples of how, when given the opportunity to spend time at Great Wood, there is never a shortage of willing participants even if they are coming to do hard labour.

'Great Wood has given so many the opportunity to experience

the countryside, a thing I have clearly taken for granted at times over the years. At Calm, on a walk up to Crowcombe Park Gate we noticed one of our group had fallen behind and was frantically taking photographs. As we waited we wondered what it was she had seen and were keen to see the photos. None of us could have guessed the answer. When she caught up, we asked what she had seen and she gave us all a stark reminder of what a privilege it is to grow up in the countryside as she replied, "It was a wild sheep." We did explain to her about the sheep grazing that occurs on the Quantocks and thankfully she joined in with the laughter.'

Another Wedding

For some people just coming to camp at Great Wood as a camper, then a team member and a leader, isn't enough. Lucy d'Orton-Gibson explains.

'I should really start by saying that Reuben and I love Great Wood. It has played a huge part in both our lives, not least because we met there in 2007 and were married there in 2015, but also because it's where we met Christian friends, learnt how to lead cabins and progressed in our own walks with God.

'This story has a heritage which starts many years before we met. Reuben's grandpa was the site manager in the 1970s and 1980s and my own mummy was a camper at Great Wood as a child before going on to cook for and lead multiple camps. Given our families' ties to this special field, it was very likely that Reuben and I would also come to love it. I started going to Great Wood as a baby as the daughter of team and have many happy memories of playing in the stream and eating extra food from the larder, while Reuben first attended GWX at the age of ten.

'Fast-forward to 2007 and Reuben maintains that we first met at Storm, the Easter camp at the time. He and a friend were mountain biking for the day and popped in to see what was going on. I have no recollection of meeting Reuben at this time, but am assured that it definitely happened. That summer we both attended The Real Thing. While I wouldn't say contact with the opposite sex was encouraged, there was an infamous meeting cleaning the toilets at the end of camp and the rest, as they say, is history. Reuben and I started officially going out at the ripe age of fourteen and would catch the coach between Poole and London to see each other at weekends.

'Eight years later, following GCSEs, A-levels and university, Reuben popped the question in the Peak District and we began to plan our wedding. As we had never lived in the same city up to this point, and as it had been a long-held dream of my own to have my wedding at camp, the obvious place to hold our wedding was at Great Wood. It held, and still holds, special significance to us personally and as a couple. We therefore began attending St Mary's Nether Stowey once a month to be legally married in the church in the village, which has a long association with camp, followed by a marquee reception in the camp field.

'We were married on the 19th of September 2015, which was thankfully sunny (a very happy answer to prayer!). The church service was led by my godfather, Roger Widdecombe, who himself was a camper at Great Wood, and our vows were conducted by John Simmons, the chair of the Great Wood Trustees and also a good family friend, so the whole service had a particularly Great Wood family feel, which we loved. Following the service in St Mary's we had ice cream and photos at the church before people headed back to camp. Ben (the farmer next door) very kindly let people park on his field; it had been temporarily connected to the Banda car park via a bridge over the stream built by Reuben's amazing Uncle Bill, to enable guests to bypass a significant walk up the road. There were drinks on the patio before dinner and lots of dancing in the marquee constructed on the lower half of the field. And, of course, no camp wedding would be complete without a camp fire (built in style by a team which included ushers and a bridesmaid and was expertly led by Reuben's cousin Joel),

Wedding venue

which, one of my non-Great-Wood-going friends remarked, reminded them of "the beacons of Gondor". It was an incredibly happy day and I am assured that the fireside fun continued long into the night, just as it has on many a camp before.

'There were many amazing things about holding our wedding reception at Great Wood, but one of my personal favourites was being able to share one of our favourite places with all the people we love! For the two of us, holding our wedding at camp only added to the significance of that particular field in our hearts.

'We continue to be involved in Great Wood through Tracks, the Easter camp, and through the newsletter, and pray that in the years to come it will continue to be a safe space for young people to grow in their relationship with God. And, one day, we look forward to sending our own children to camps at Great Wood.'

A Place for Family

'It has been long established that there is a Great Wood family made up of any and all who have attended the site,' Joel Carter writes, 'but there is now a long list of families that have been born out of Great Wood and for whom it holds a very special place in their lives. Pat and Mike Owen, Peter and Jen Hudson, Bill and Elizabeth Carter, Simon and Esther Culy, Hilda and Mike Menzies, Joel and Stephanie Carter, Reuben and Lucy d'Orton-Gibson, Gill and Peter Hollis, and David and Janice Morris are just some of those who met at Great Wood and subsequently married. And they in turn have brought their children and grandchildren to camp.'

A young work party trainee sporting some promotional attire

Estate Managers

Andy Bennett is the latest member in the line of hard-working, behind-the-scenes estate managers. The role varies enormously depending on what is happening on site, from seeing groups in or out to making sure there will be enough crockery, cutlery, cleaning materials and even pillows on site for each camp, to keeping an eye on contractors, to collecting cream cakes and doughnuts from a certain bakery for the nourishment of working parties, and lots more. It is hard to give a picture of what it is like, but what follows, in his own words, will both be enlightening and provide fuel for our prayers.

'I took over from Gerry in the closed season of 2009–10, and initially shadowed him for a season. I had already done his job as a temporary thing whilst he and Clare had gone to Singapore for nine months in 2006. I was first employed as estate manager for six days a month (averaged out over the fiscal year).

'The start of my tenure was interesting with the resignation of Gilbert Villis, local builder, from his post three days later! He gave me a ten-minute walk around the site as my handover. Fortunately Gerry, being the generous-spirited man that he is, was on hand to answer any questions – indeed I said to him lately that I could not have done this job without his friendship, support and extensive knowledge (and wise counsel).

'John Simmons and the trustees then asked me if I was willing to combine the roles of managing and repairing ... and initially I was trying to do all of it in six days a month. It was possible whilst Gerry was still in post, but once it was all down to me, it quickly became obvious that to do a good job I would need more time, and so after a couple of hectic seasons my contract was extended to ten days a month (averaged over the fiscal year).'

More about the Mess Hut

John Simmons recalls the trustees having long and detailed discussions with SU about the mess hut beginning in 2010. It was clear that they were not in a position to raise the money needed for a quality replacement building, and we were not able to ask for funds to build on someone else's land on the back of a three-year licence agreement. So all agreed that the right course of action would be for the Great Wood Trust to buy the freehold for the site from SU.

This sounds simple, but there were two major complications. First, SU believed it had a duty to obtain best value from a sale. Secondly, the savings we had in the trust at that stage had been earmarked for the mess hut.

The first complication took a long time to address, and involved many meetings and discussions with SU. One problem arose because SU had decided to appoint a firm of solicitors who specialised in planning matters. They reported in July 2011 with the prospect that the site could be sold for development as a holiday park, and consequently there was hope value in addition to its value for its existing use. SU wrestled with this for some time, and were eventually persuaded that the negative publicity which would arise from testing the potential through the planning process would irreparably damage our relationship with the locals, with Kilve, and with our dedicated band of Great Wood folk.

SU then had to address the situation where, if change of use could be secured, the site would be worth some £700,000, whereas we had agreed, with the invaluable help of Francis Darrah, that the existing use value was £450,000. The dilemma was eventually overcome by our agreeing with SU that, should the site ever be sold for development (heaven forbid!), any surplus value would be handed back to them.

But if it's the right thing, the Lord provides the answer. The finally agreed purchase price of £450,000 was funded by SU being granted a six-year licence to use the site for summer holidays without charge, by our accumulated savings of £80,000, and by a ten-year loan from the Slavanka Trust, interest-free, to be forgiven annually provided the ministry continues as at present. (The Slavanka Trust has for some years supported SU camping ministry across the world, and had agreed to work with us in partnership.)

Finally, in August 2014, the freehold was transferred to GWT, and we were free to continue with the mess hut project.

Having used all our savings on the purchase, we turned our attention to raising the money for the project. It never fails to amaze us how God provides. Sometimes, in the Western world, the question 'how much will it cost?' comes too early in the process. The Lord knows what we need, and, if we have correctly understood His mind, He does provide, and at the right time.

Psalm 127:1 says, 'If God doesn't build the house, the builders only build shacks' (*The Message*). At each step of the journey, when we had wobbles as to whether we were doing the right thing, the Lord gave us clear and sometimes amazing encouragement, such that, by autumn 2016, we were in a position to advise Kilve that during autumn 2017 and spring 2018 the site would become a building site and therefore not be available to them.

When we signed the contract with local builders Harris Bros & Collard in June 2017, we had sufficient cash and promises in hand to be assured of being able to pay the full £685,000 contract figure. To this we added £25,000 for furnishings and the conversion of Eve to a drying room and laundry, work which Andy is completing at the time of writing.

Demolition and Rebuild of the Mess Hut

'Without doubt the hardest project has been the preparing of the site for the demolition of the mess hut,' Andy Bennett writes. 'It should have been so easy, and I had a timeline and a plan which made it look achievable. However, it quickly became obvious when dealing with service companies (gas, electricity, telephone etc.) that they had their own agenda, speed for delivery and so on, so what started as a six-month job quickly escalated to fifteen months of phone calls, hair tearing, teeth gnashing and feeling insignificant as a mere customer! The change of route for the main electrical cable into site is a good example.

'The trustees announced at the December meeting of 2015 that the planning permission was due to expire in June 2016 unless a "substantial start" could be initiated, and I was instructed to investigate and to instigate the cable rerouting project as soon as possible, to be completed by the end of February 2016 in time for when the Easter work party came into camp!

A start is made: taking down the tractor shed

'I contacted Western Power Distribution (WPD) and discussed the project with their surveyor and planning chap – who was very helpful, but didn't think it was achievable in the time frame available. Several site meetings took place and costs were estimated, using a conversion to the existing rubbish shed at the entrance next to the LPG tank as the site for the new meter.

'I thought that I should check that using this existing shed would count as a "substantial start", and was dismayed to find out from the architects that it would not. A complete new building had to be put up.

'So Plan A was abandoned and a brand new electricity plant room (shed) was designed, and costs approved by the trustees. The building footings were dug, and the process began of costing the route of the cable again. Meanwhile, the contractor who was building the plant room was unavoidably unavailable for three months. Work party 2016 came and went before I finally got the contractor to come back and hurriedly finish the job.

'I had been in constant contact with our chosen electrical contractors throughout this process, and many site meetings with them took place, but there were still some unresolved issues.

'The building shell was finished, lovely but empty! I clad the outside with timber and the roof was completed with cedar tiles to match the cabins. This was about ten days before the planning permission expired – phew!

'The day of the connection reroute was scheduled for early December 2016, and so during November I spent some weeks with a contractor digging, tracing and mapping the water and electricity cables, which spread out from the old mess hut in a tangle of directions to various buildings on site. As there was no accurate existing plan I had several meetings and calls to Gerry before we managed to trace and identify the various cables and pipes. Some of the water pipes had been installed literally just below the grass level, and so we "found" and had to repair two live water pipes in the first sweep of the digger. Remember that the reconnection had to be made whilst keeping the building and all services live for one more season (2017).

'The day before the reconnection date, I had a last-minute meeting at site with the contractor and WPD surveyor to confirm that the new route agreed was entirely within our boundary, and I watched as it was marked up in blue paint on the afternoon before the job was to be done.

'I had also been in negotiation with the Forestry Commission throughout the planning process, as we might have needed to dig up their road (the Forestry chap claimed that six months' notice was not really sufficient), and so I was particularly pleased to achieve a route which would not involve touching the Forestry Commission road surface at all.

'On the day of the actual reroute I was unable to be present but received a phone call from an irate Forestry Commission ranger telling me that the WPD contractors had dug a 2.5-metre trench across the forest track and that they had no permission etc. I managed to control my temper and referred him to the WPD control centre!

'When I next went to camp I found that our own electrical contractors had bypassed the £600 drawpit and simply drilled a hole in the floor of the new plant room. They had also laid two new cables over the top of existing water pipes with insufficient clearance as required by building regulations, so I had to get our plumber to come and reroute the water pipes under the new electrical cables.

'Our electrical contractors had also been tasked with running a new cable along the bank behind the existing mess hut to the JI hut power board, but when I went to check this had been done, I saw that they had simply run the cable around the old mess hut building and installed an external joint box on the wall of the drying room – which was due to be demolished!

'The whole process took about seventeen months from start to finish, and this was just the electrical side. Whilst this was all

The new switch house

taking place I also had to trace and reroute the two existing water supplies, the LPG and the telephone (don't get me started on the telephone issues; that's a whole other chapter!).'

This lengthy description will give an idea of the frustrations that Andy had to face whilst overseeing a very small part of the total project.

Letting the Site to Other Groups

'We have had everything from wedding parties to birthday parties, family groups and large "whole" church weekends,' Andy writes. 'We have had a French group, two Polish groups, and many youth clubs … the list goes on. We have had a "Dads and Lads" football group and a group of children who have been excluded from school. We have many returning church groups from around the south and west, and some faces whom I see year after year.'

Patrick Weld has been the Great Wood chaplain since 2013. His love for the Lord, his integrity, his infectious good humour and his approachability mean that he is wonderfully suited to the role. He works closely with the staff of Kilve Court (who oversee the schools work on site) and plays a part in the weekly activities of all the residentials. Typically, he will be on hand to greet schools when they arrive, he will run an assembly during the week and he will be involved in some of the walks and activities. His storytelling is extremely popular! During the winter months, Patrick makes contact with the schools, visits them and runs discussions and group activities with the pupils.

The importance of what Patrick does cannot be overestimated and his ministry is showing real fruit: schools are requesting more input from him into their programmes and there is a genuine openness to Christianity. This is something new and is very exciting.

The following 'miniatures', in Patrick's own words, give a flavour of his work.

'One of the things that I most like to ask staff when they come away is if they have seen a different side to the children. The answer so far has always been "yes", but the variety of reasons why is fascinating. Quite often it's along the lines of "Little Timmy struggles in class and is constantly naughty, but at Great Wood, with the space and activity, he has become a different boy, and an unexpectedly brilliant leader."

'One staff member gave a different response once, which has stayed with me ever since. She pointed out one boy who was enthusiastically playing football with his mates and had been loving the time away, and said that at school he was like a goldfish.

'"A goldfish?" I questioned.

'"Yes, he sits there doing not very much and just stares at you with a blank expression." She then did her best impression of a goldfish, vacant stare, opening and closing her mouth. "But here, he's come alive! It's wonderful."

'"Why do you think that is?" I asked.

'"Well, at home, nobody cares. He goes home and cooks his own dinner, then goes to his room and plays *Minecraft* until 3am every night. When he finally gets up in the morning he has no breakfast and so comes in late, tired and hungry. You can't learn much when you're in that state. But on camp there are no electronics, he gets fed three times a day, is made to go to bed at a sensible time and the staff care about him, so he is a different boy. You can see the real him, his personality has come out."

'I honestly didn't know whether to be happy or sad: happy that this boy was spending a precious week experiencing life in its fullness, and he was certainly having the time of his life, or sad that the week was coming to an end and he'd be returning to his previous existence. My hope and prayer for that little boy was that his memories of life at camp would have a lasting impact on him, and help him to seek better for himself.'

Rick Astley

'A couple of years ago,' Patrick remembers, 'an instructor called Ollie and I were leading a walk of about thirty kids through the forest on a pleasant summer's day. We were chatting happily with the kids at the front about many a meandering subject. We got onto the topic of favourite singers and when someone mentioned a male singer, one of the kids pitched in with a comment about there being no good lead male singers. "Not so!" replied another boy. "You've got lots of great lead singers. Bands like AC/DC, Metallica, Guns N' Roses, Rick Astley ..."

'Ollie and I looked at each other and burst out laughing. Going from three iconic metal bands to Rick Astley was funny enough, but the kid was ten years old. How had he even heard of Rick Astley? Needless to say, that boy became one of our favourite campers of the week. I forget his real name now, because we just called him Rick from then on.'

First Week on the Job

In his first week on the job, Patrick was actually quite upset. 'Don't misunderstand me; I felt that I had been led by the Lord from my old role and brought to this one. I was thankful for the Lord's guidance and his provision, and I looked forward to all that was to come. At the same time, however, I had spent almost seven years as chaplain to a school that I loved very much, and leaving the kids was a tremendous wrench. I think it is fair to say that I went through a grieving period, such was the difficulty of leaving the old school behind.

'As I was driving to the site one particular morning I was finding it very hard. We were sorting the camp out ready for the first arrivals the next week, but having gone from being in the heart of 550ish kids to having no relationships with any, and having to start again, it was one of those mornings. I remember telling Jesus that I was finding it hard, and that it was a struggle that day, more than it had been on others.

'As I crossed the cattle grid I started trying to pull myself together to try and appear normal when I pulled into the car park. As I got out of my car I paused a moment to look around the site, and then and there God showed me something so beautiful it seemed entirely for my benefit. There was a low-hanging mist in the trees, and the sun was just cresting the hill behind the tallest of them. The shafts of light through the mist, which were split by the branches, were just spectacular on this still spring morning. I'm sure if you've spent time at the site in the early morning you'll have seen something similar. But it was so special to me, a little pick-me-up from the Lord in a difficult time. It was, to me, as if the Lord was saying, "I know it's tough now, but it'll be OK." It's hard to put into words how much that little moment meant to me, and the difference that it made, but that is the grace of God to us as Christians, and it is a wonderful thing.'

Sunlight through the trees

Wasps' Nest

'In the first summer term at camp there was a slight issue with a number of wasps building nests around the site. I had never seen a wasps' nest before, but the papery balls sprang up in a number of places,' Patrick writes. 'Some of them were fine and would be no trouble, but there was one being made under the eaves of the pool cabin, right in front of the front door. This one would be no good, and had to go. I think that Andy Bennett might usually deal with them, he is that kind of guy, but for some reason he was not around. Carly, the manager for the local authority, was saying that she'd have to call someone up to get it dealt with.

'Being ever game for a challenge, I said that there was no need to call anyone; I'd sort it out. It was in the face of raised eyebrows and "you do it at your own risk" comments that I started to gather the things I needed. A handful of straw and some paper for a fire, an old metal mop bucket to hold it in, and some green grass to create a good amount of smoke. The final thing that I needed was a good

154

stick with which to eliminate the nest itself, which I found in the wood store. It was a thick log, which had about the same circumference as the wasps' nest, and I thought that after I'd administered a good amount of smoke to make them drowsy, one swift bash should suffice. Quick, clean and safe.

'Carly and the two trainee instructors stood up by Cabin 3, not wanting to take any chances themselves, and looked on with interest to see what might unfold. I lit the fire, put the green grass on top and waited for it to start smoking, then I held the mop bucket up underneath the nest and allowed a good amount of time for the wasps to get really drowsy. Then the moment came to put the bucket down and pick up the log. No chickening out! No hesitating! Manly!

'I prepared for my decisive victory and took a deep breath. I hit the nest pretty hard, but in that moment fear overtook me and thoughts of huge clouds of angry wasps filled my mind. Throwing all machismo to the wind, I dropped everything and ran as fast as I could towards the sanctuary of the other three. I don't think I squealed, but I couldn't promise. Supportive as they were, they began waving and cheering, and shouting something which I could not make out. As I got closer I realised that they were waving me away from them and shouting to go anywhere but where they were. *With friends like these,* I thought, as I wheeled away from them and towards the mess hut for refuge . . .

'When I dared to slow a little I discovered no wasps on my tail, and upon returning cautiously to the nest it was clear that I had done a pretty decent job with my first blow. Happy with the effort, I returned to the group, expecting a pat on the back maybe, some congratulatory words, admiration even. I expected too much! As anyone who has worked in a jovial place will have come to know, the currency is humour and all I got was a ribbing for how I'd bolted. It was the blossoming of friendships, which later allowed me to share my faith with the staff, and speak with them numerous times about God, life and all those little things that mean a lot.

'There are many things that I could say, and stories that I could tell, but these are a few that epitomise my experience working at Great Wood. For those who know God, His presence is tangible there. For those that don't, they tend to describe it as a place that feels *nice, peaceful, special*. It is all those things. I feel privileged to have my role, and to be able to serve the schools and staff. I try to help in whatever way I can, be that leading a session of archery or unblocking the drains. Doing so and spending time with the schools builds those relationships, and relationships are key to then being able to tell them a story at the last night's camp fire. Knowing a school better helps me to select a story that fits with their journey and what is happening in their lives. You can pick up a feel from the children and staff, and so tailor the story for the needs of the group. As they get to know me too, they are more willing to listen to the story and engage with it. I am not just a random person telling fables, but someone they know and trust, and the story has a meaning which is important. I always like to finish by telling the children that I am a Christian, that I believe in God and Jesus, and I tell them what Jesus said about the subject of the story. This way they know that the story is rooted in the Bible and Jesus, and is not just good intentions and fuzzy feelings. When we get children who return it is always encouraging hearing that they have remembered the story from the year before and even better if they can remember the point too!'

Country Dancing

Many hundreds of people have enjoyed an evening or several evenings of country dancing over the years. It provides an environment which helps break down barriers amidst a lot of laughter. So it was no real surprise that the work party of 2016 should stage such a dance to celebrate two significant birthdays, Clare Nichols' and Bill Carter's. The Weaver family kindly provided the music and instruction.

The Weaver Country Dance Band

International Connections

John Simmons recounts that after the trust was formed in 2007, the trustees continued the practice set up by GWEG of providing a fund to SU Europe for the provision of subsidies for campers in Eastern Europe who cannot afford the fees. More recently, the Slavanka Trust has helped us with this, and some of the stories arising from our connection with a wider ministry are truly heart-warming.

Here's one from Lithuania:

'Thanks to the special summer grant we were able to support five campers and two volunteers.

'Eimantas, who is thirteen now, has been coming to our camps for many years. As a child he would always misbehave and be a great challenge to the leaders. He would run away, make silly faces or comments during worship time and try to break a lot of camp rules. We already noticed how his behaviour got better last year and that he started respecting everything at the camp more. However, this summer Eimantas was very interested in the Bible. He got to respect his roommates – even made their beds one morning. Most importantly, Eimantas prayed the prayer asking Christ to come into his life.

'After the camp one of our volunteer counsellors met Eimantas' grandmother in the city. Grandmother said that Eimantas is very intrigued by the New Testament. He reads it every day and asks his grandmother questions. His younger sister, who also comes to our camps, joins him in reading the New Testament.'

In 2017 Scripture Union International became interested in developing its worldwide ministry to those with a disability. Jan Simmons was asked to join a working group with others from Canada, India, Nigeria, Australia, Estonia, France and Serbia. All had different approaches and models but were of one heart in developing this ministry. As a result a guidance manual was issued at the 150th Anniversary SU Global Conference in Kuala Lumpur in November. The Great Wood Wide Open Holiday was one of the models given, and Jan is an advisor for other movements around the world that might want to set up a similar ministry.

The New Mess Hut

'At the time of printing, perhaps the biggest building project in the history of camp is under way,' Bill Carter writes. 'The new mess hut will allow greater ease of access for the physically less able. It will bring a level of comfort to the main building not previously experienced, which will enable us to extend the season to the end of November. It will combine all the add-ons to the original mess hut in one purpose-built structure whilst removing those bits that have become redundant. It will have improved catering facilities

New mess hut

and will blend in well. But the main benefit will be realised as the teams of people come and learn how to make the most of the facilities to share God's love in the twenty-first century. There will be teething problems and there will be plenty of work for the work party and Andy Bennett in turning the new structure into the new mess hut. It is very exciting.'

Conclusion

The final word goes to Gill Hollis.

'As with so many other people, Great Wood became a part of me from the first time I saw it. I never went on any other SU camps. It wasn't just the site, the smell of the pine forest and creosote, the rope over the stream, the lanterns in the cabins, the country dancing and the friendships made. Of course, I returned time and time again because of the presence of God. I learned so much about

Him at each and every camp. Enough to keep me going from one year to the next (I did not attend the most exciting of churches). Enough to shape my life and my attitudes and relationships. Enough to make me the person I am. Enough that I can never sing "How Great Thou Art" without being transported back to a clearing in the Quantock forest. And knowing that when Christ shall come, with shout of acclamation, to take me home, I will be there with all these wonderful Great Wood friends who have loved me and nurtured me, wept and rejoiced with me for over forty years.'

'Then sings my soul, my Saviour God, to Thee, how great Thou art.'

Appendix 1: Timeless Bits

―⦿―

Camp Song

Dr C Thorton Weekley, known to all and sundry as Docco, with his wife were great friends of the camp in the early days. They were the parents of Lynette, one of the previously mentioned and highly esteemed cooks. Dorothy Weekley's brothers were JB Phillips and Kenneth Phillips who, as a family, made a most worthy contribution to practical evangelical religious faith. Lynette's father was no exception. He wrote the extremely evocative words and music for the camp song. It is a proper Great Wood song as the first and last groups of 'Hullos' imitate the blowing of a huntsman's horn. Here are the words of the song in full,

> *Hullo-o, hullo-o, hullo-o!*
> *Pray welcome be;*
> *And feel quite free*
> *To breathe this rare*
> *Unrationed air,*
> *To climb the trees*
> *Just as you please,*
> *Or laze around*
> *Upon the ground,*
> *Or stand instead*
> *Upon your head.*
> *Or, if you're one who likes to shiver*
> *Pray take a dip within the river!*
> *So hot and dry, or cold and damp,*
> *Be warmly hailed to Great Wood Camp.*
> *Hullo-o, hullo-o, hullo-o!*

Docco Weekley wrote a camp acrostic, too, in the form of a prayer which was printed on an address list in 1960:

God, Who reveald'st Thy love on Calvary's Tree,
Reveal, amid these trees, Thy love to me –
Each tree-crowned hill proclaiming Calvary.
Among these fields, beside this murmuring rill,
Thy lambs, Good Shepherd, seek for life indeed.

With living Water thirsty ones now fill,
On heavenly Food our hungry spirits feed.
Open our eyes, Thou Sunshine from above,
Dawn in our hearts with warmth and light and love.

Come, Wind of God, blow clear our souls of wrong.
Around this camp fire fan our hearts to flame.
Men may we be, courageous, true and strong,
Proud 'neath our flag to fight in Jesus' Name.

There was also a camp hymn – 'How Great Thou Art'. The second verse was altered and made more fitting for the camps at which it was sung. The altered second verse is as follows,

When through the woods and forest glades I wander
And see the deer move nimbly through the trees:
When I look down from lofty hillside grandeur,
And hear the stream, and feel the rushing breeze.

And so the camp was well catered for, and we are especially grateful to the Weekleys.

David Fieldsend reminds us of the reasons for the changes to 'How Great Thou Art'. John Inchley felt it was ridiculous to hear a brook from a mountain top, especially when competing with a rushing breeze. He also felt deer to be more special to Great Wood than birds. In the Great Wood version of verse four, John also felt that

'When Christ shall come ... to claim His own' was a bit less presumptuous than 'When Christ shall come ... and take me home'.

Newsletters

There was a series of three-monthly newsletters which began at Christmas in 1952 and lasted, apparently, until the summer term in 1964. Their object was to encourage a most real fellowship amongst the Great Wood campers, though there was always a motivation for those who were old enough to attend other Scripture Union camps. These newsletters always contained spiritual pages and details of reunions while the remainder of the short space, contained in a single folded A4 sheet, was given over to camp news and light-hearted nonsense. The camp news invariably boosted the Scripture Union method of daily Bible reading and gave the name and address of the camps' SU secretary. For many years this was the faithful Brian Stanley, who was an original camper at Great Wood from Monkton Combe. Later on he attended the camps as an older boy, and a much valued helper.

Reading through the available newsletters which have survived, it is most interesting to notice that postage on a card in 1953 was only 2d in old money, and that sweets became unrationed after the Second Great War in that same year.

The Great Wood newsletter continues to be published on a regular basis, and is available either electronically or by post.

Cost

The cost of the camps in the early days is not without interest. For example, in 1944 for nine days it was less than £2.50 while as late as 1968 for eleven days it was £9.00 with £1.00 extra for excursions. Prices, necessarily, have risen somewhat since those good old days.

In 2017 Wide Open, which is perhaps the most expensive per person per night because of its specialist nature, was £180 for a five-day camp, whilst the work party gave best value for money at just £32.50 for four and a half days.

Equipment

The equipment purchased for the camp was always of the very best quality. In the very early days of the project I was travelling on a London bus, of all places, and found myself puzzled by the excellent quality of the materials used in its total construction. Eventually it was borne home to me that this was essential if daily deterioration was effectively to be withstood. The outcome of this experience was to purchase only the very best equipment for the camp and to wait in order to do so, should the necessary cash not be readily available. It is a policy which over and over again has proved to be the right one.

… and the Great Wood trustees would say, 'Hear, hear!' We continue to believe that we should be offering the very best experience to the children and young people who come to camp.

The Blue Butcher

Of course, as is to be expected, Great Wood always had its own ghost while Jack Belcher, who was a man of many parts, and regularly came to the camps as a senior helper, would impersonate this ghost quite realistically whenever there was a night game at the camp. Fortunately for the campers, they already knew who it was, so that his powers of scaring the boys who took part in the activity when it was dark were greatly diminished. Nevertheless it always added a sparkle to the game as one never knew where Jack was, and he would just appear making weird noises! The ghost hauntingly called the Blue Butcher was a pirate, so the story relates, who used to live in a house just above the camp. This Blue Butcher had a habit of receiving contraband landing on the coast, not many miles away, and was killed on a significant occasion, after an argument, by one of his own racketeers. The cottage he occupied has since been rebuilt, and now has electricity, but is still extremely remote. Notwithstanding, the Blue Butcher, so it is said, still roams the forest in the vicinity of his old home although, as far as I know, he has never been seen!

Appendix 2: Significant Dates

—◦⟨◦⟩◦—

1943   First Scout camp under John Inchley.

1944   First VPS summer camp in tents. Cost £2 7s 6d for nine days.

1945   Easter camp at Over Stowey WI.
        Idea born of permanent camp.
        Second VPS summer camp in tents. Dilys Gething cooked out-of-doors.
        Purchase of Nissen hut in the autumn for £60.

1945/46 Permission granted by local council to build on field.
        Agreement of the farmer to let the field be used as a permanent camp.
        Nissen hut erected on field at a cost of £240.

1946   Twelve sleeping cabins purchased from the War Office at a cost of £7 10s each.
        Easter boys' camp April 9–16.
        First summer VPS camp using Nissen hut and sleeping cabins.
        Well dug behind Old 10 to supply drinking water and used until 1949.

1947   Old swimming pool dug and used.
        Fireplace and chimney erected in Nissen hut.

1949   Pipeline laid for water – hand pump installed.

1951   First camp for girls under the leadership of Mrs RT Archibald.
        Middle hut and shop erected.

1953   Purchase of the freehold of the site from the neighbouring farmer, Mr Tucker, for £300.
        Alteration and enlargement of sleeping cabins.
        Derek Joy and Peter Stanford build lean-to behind

	Nissen hut in the Christmas holidays.
	New toilet block erected and Elsan toilets and cold taps installed.
	Vardo presented to JI.
1954	Christmas camp under leadership of David Gardiner.
	Model of camp presented to JI by Brocksford Hall Prep School.
1955	Installation of petrol pump for water.
1956	Erection of new flag mast.
	Erection of new gate with wagon wheels.
1958	Opening of new swimming pool (two and a half times bigger than old one) at a cost of £259.
	Installation of new water pipeline from well above camp in the forest.
	Building of water tower.Gift of water closets.
1959	Purchase of additional land from Mr Bartlett for £60.
1960	Chimney collapses almost to the day when it was built in 1947.
1962	New mess hut erected at a cost of £3,750.
	Chapel furnished at a cost of £250.
1963	New mess hut officially opened by Sir Alfred Owen.
	Septic tank and new WCs installed.
1964	New forestry road built.
1965	New sleeping cabins.
1969	Rosemary and Paul Watson's wedding reception.
1971	JI and Mrs I with family say goodbye to Great Wood but are more than glad the camp is to continue under the Scripture Union banner.
1972/3	JI hut built at a cost of £4,012.
1976	Stainless steel sinks and draining boards fitted throughout kitchen and outside washup.
1980	Swimming pool number three built and commissioned with filter system.
	Boot porch added to mess hut.

1981/2   Toilet block (Adam & Eve) revamped with improved workshop space, £8,842.

1983/4   New bosun's store built at a cost of £4,572.

1984   Major land drainage project.

1987   Pressurised water system installed to eliminate(?!) airlocks. Still fed from spring up the combe.

1988   Shower block added to mess hut, £27,189.
         Banda upgraded with larger kitchen and bathroom.

1989   Electricity comes to the sleeping cabins.

1989/90   New 10 (chapel cabin) built to replace Old 10, £9,974.

1991/2   New 1 (pool cabin), £12,171.

1991/2   Tractor shed, £1,613.

1993   Office added to kitchen end of mess hut, £6,707.

1996   Mains water arrives on site.

1996/7   Gate cabin, £19,076.

1999   Drying room added to boot porch end of mess hut, £5,494.
         Central heating installed in mess hut.

2000   Low ropes course constructed in area behind New 10.

2002   New electricity supply.
         Extension to chapel cabin, £8,730 (this enabled use by disabled campers).

2003   Extension to pool cabin, £13,492.

2003   Extension to gate cabin, £10,595.

2004   Six new log cabins built, £45,000 each. Five of the old cabins dismantled and given to an emerging Christian camp in Essex.
         JI hut remodelled and porch added.

2006/7   Electricity supply buried in ground (had been over head supply).
         New swimming pool (number four).
         Biodigester installed to replace septic tank.

2013   Planning permission granted for new mess hut.

2014   Purchase of site by GWT.

2017/18   New mess hut – estimated cost £800,000.

Appendix 3:
List of Contributors

John Axford, camper and leader from 1950s

Andy Bennett, estate manager from 2009

Lesley Blight, head of Scripture Union in Schools 1991 to 1995, field director 1996 to 2008

Michael Briggs, son of Derek Briggs, LEA warden

Bill Carter, camper and leader from 1967

Elizabeth Carter (née Gibson), camper and team from 1969

Joel Carter, camper and leader from 1990s

Margaret Ferguson (née Buchanan), girls' camp leader in 1970s

David Fieldsend, camper and team from 1960s

Sylvia Fox, camper and team from 1976 to mid-1980s

Matushka Sarah Gascoigne (née Frances Turner), camper, early 1960s

Mary Gladstone, cook from 1947 until 1968

Anthony Greenhill, team from 1954 to 1963 and from 2001

Gill Hollis (née Wood), camper and team from 1975

Jen Hudson (née Sisley), camper and team from 1974

Judy Hunt, leader of girls' camp in 1980s

Steve and Judy Hutchinson, leaders and SU workers

John Inchley (deceased), author of *The Great Wood Story* (Scripture Union, 1990) and founder of Great Wood Camp

Sue Keighley (née Nicholls), camper and leader from 1970s and trustee of GWT

John Langford, camper and team from 1952

Berta Lawrence, author of *Quantock Country* (Westaway, 1952)

Alan Martin (deceased), co-author of *The Great Wood Story*

(Scripture Union, 1990), camp leader and estate manager, worked for SU until 1991

Mike Menzies, camper and team from 1960s

Jan(ice) Morris,(nee Baines) camper and team from 1969

Ruth Nicholls, mother of Sue Keighley

Lucy d'Orton-Gibson (née Keighley), camper and team from 2000s

Rev. Chris Owen, camper and leader from 1970s

John Owen, camper and leader from 1960s and trustee of GWT

Michael Owen, one of the first campers and lifelong helper and supporter

Carol Phillips, Mrs I's daughter

Mary Rennison, leader from 2004 and trustee of GWT

Jan Simmons, camper and leader from 1960s and trustee of GWT

John Simmons, leader from 1970s and trustee of GWT

Jane Sutton, team member from 1950s

Paul Vines, camper and team member, 1990 to 2006

Rosemary Watson, daughter of JI

Elizabeth Weaver (née Cunningham), camper and team from 1960s

Patrick Weld, chaplain of Great Wood from 2013

David Whitehouse, camper and team from 1968 and trustee of GWT

Ed Wicke, team at work party

Lightning Source UK Ltd.
Milton Keynes UK
UKHW02f0330130418
320992UK00002B/9/P